I now have...

1,099 DAILY

Affirmations

FOR SELF-CHANGE

By: Janet D. Swerdlow

I always attract...

I love myself...

I release the need...

Copyright © 2010 Expansions Publishing Company, Inc.

Cover design, typography and book layout: Lorraine Sarich
www.lorrainecsarich.com

For further information, contact:

Published by: Expansions Publishing Company, Inc.
                 P.O. Box 12
                 Saint Joseph MI 49085 USA
                 PH: 269-429-8615
                 FX: 269-429-8616

ISBN# 978-0-9740144-2-5

website address: www.expansions.com
email: janet@expansions.com

Dedication

To Stewart, my beloved husband,
who continually inspires me to
become a better person.

Contents

Introduction to Affirmations

Affirmation: A statement that defines a course of action, or a state of inner being; repeating words many times by thinking, speaking, or writing them to bring new avenues of action into your conscious mind.

You use affirmations every day, whether you are consciously aware of this or not. You consistently and constantly affirm your state of being in the present moment as well as set the course of your future. For example:

I never have enough time.
If you never have enough, how do you expect abundance to come to you?

I can't stand it.
If you can't stand, what does this say about your support structures in life?

I am sick about what happened.
If you are sick, how can you be healthy?

I am broken-hearted over what he did to me.
How can a broken heart hold healthy emotions?

I never get what I want.
How can you ever get what you want?

I am so stupid!
How can you be intelligent?

Every year I get a cold.
How can you expect to be healthy next year?

People always let me down.
How can you ever develop supportive relationships?

Listen to your words and what you affirm every day. Do you affirm the positive or the negative? What expressions do you repeatedly use? What do they suggest about your inner state of being?

Affirmations are really about consciously choosing the words that you think and speak about your inner state of being. These words consist of color, tone, and archetype (symbol) that set your life up as you speak each and every word. By directing your words, you can consciously create the life that you want to live. You can purposefully direct the flow of your life.

Of course, first you have to recognize what you have already unconsciously created. Then, you have to redirect what you have already set in motion—and this is where life gets bumpy. You dismantle the old foundation to rebuild a new one. This transition process can be a bit of a challenge. The old way does not fit anymore but the new way is not all in place yet. You may even wonder if you are making the best choices and decisions.

The old way is comfortable because you know it. The new way is not comfortable simply because you do not know this new path. You are learning. Have patience with yourself. Transition takes time. Think about the inner needs that the old way fulfilled. Think about what the new path has to offer when it is successfully completed.

Use your words as tools to create your world. If it takes longer to create your world than you would like, there is a reason. As you change, your goals and desires change. Time gives you a chance to refine and re-define what it is you truly want as your end goal. What you thought you wanted yesterday may not be what you want today or tomorrow.

Be patient and kind with yourself. You are worth the time. You deserve the best. You deserve to understand the life that you now live, how you got there, what you want to keep, what you are ready to discard, and what you want to create.

Your words are powerful tools that with conscious direction motivate and move you exactly where you need to be. Appreciate the process of reaching your goals, however long it takes. What you do with these word tools is all up to you. You are responsible for your life—how you got there, where you are now, and where you are going. Consciously choose your words to consciously direct your life. Start right now in this moment and your life changes forever. The power that you hold is amazingly astounding!

Abandonment

Day One

Many people have abandonment issues. Abandonment issues are expressed in many different ways. Often, people feel abandonment in early childhood by a parent, or even a sibling, either physically or emotionally—and sometimes both. Abandonment is also felt by those who are adopted, lost a loved one through death, and/or somehow been involved in divorce. Do you have any such feelings of abandonment by anyone in your family? If so, this is the time to begin your release work.

I release any feelings of family abandonment.

Day Two

Do you have abandonment issues from friends who no longer fit into your life? People who have moved on, do not return phone calls, letters, and/or emails, "forget" important days in your life, etc. How many ways have friends abandoned you? Do you still hold onto these feelings? If so, let them go. On the Oversoul level, ask that any psychic cords from you to them, or vice versa be blessed, cleaned up, and released back to their rightful owners via the involved Oversouls.

I release all psychic cords that hold feelings of abandonment.

Day Three

Do finances and material possessions abandon you? What part of you feels that you cannot hold onto money? What part of you does not feel worthy of allowing finances and material possessions to stay with you? What part of you feels the need to keep struggling for these things?

I release the need for finances to abandon me.

Day Four

How is your health? Does optimum health abandon you? Do you have major health issues with which you are dealing, or a continual series of small issues? Do you have chronic issues or seasonal ones, such as colds and allergies? Do you have access to the kind of healthcare that you desire?

I release the need for optimum health to abandon me.

Day Five

What about your ideals and goals? What were they and what are they? Have they changed and how? Do you feel like you have abandoned your original ideals and goals, or that they have abandoned you? Or, have you simply changed? Take some time to evaluate current ideals and goals.

I release the need for my ideals and goals to abandon me.

Day Six

Do you feel that opportunities abandon you? Do you see others with opportunities that you wish were yours? Have you actually seen opportunities that for some reason do not manifest in the way you envisioned? Does your mind-pattern support bringing opportunities to yourself?

I release the need for opportunities to abandon me.

Day Seven

Do you now feel, or have you ever felt, abandoned by your Oversoul and God-Mind? Have you ever asked questions that seem to go unanswered? Have you felt alone without spiritual comfort or solace? Has your spirit felt disregarded, insignificant, and separate from its source?

I release the need to feel abandoned by my Oversoul and God-Mind.

I release the need for abandonment.

Abundance

Day One
What do you lack? Sleep? Relationships? Money? Satisfying employment? Enough closet space? Willpower? Peace and quiet? Time? What do you lack?
I identify the areas in my life that are lacking.

Day Two
The mind-pattern behind "lack" is low self-esteem, low self-worth, and feeling that you do not deserve. What part of you holds onto lack? Why?
I release the need for lack.

Day Three
Do you lack money? What is the state of your finances? Money represents the amount of God-Mind that you allow to flow in and through your life. If you attract bills, then you can attract the mind-pattern that brings you the money to pay them.
I am grateful for my bills and the funds to pay them.

Day Four
Pay attention to your words. Think about how you use your words to limit yourself. How often do you say such words as, "I never have enough sleep, enough time, and/or enough peace and quiet"? Reverse these words and statements that indicate "lack" in your life. Know that you always have "enough" of everything.
I always have enough.

Day Five
Feel yourself floating in the river of God-Mind Abundance. Feel the flow of that river moving into your body through your fingers and toes, and flowing into every fiber of your being.
Abundance flows in all areas of my life.

Day Six

As you move through your day, consciously keep in your mind, and feel in your body and soul, the flow of God-Mind Abundance. Recognize that you are connected, that you deserve to be connected, and nothing can stop you from maintaining that connection.

My life connects to the flow of abundance.

Day Seven

Focus on opening your cellular structure to hold more God-Mind Abundance. Visualize your cells becoming lighter and more free-flowing, with increased space between cells. Know that you are the only one who can stop the flow, and only you can keep the flow going.

*Limitless God-Mind abundance flows through my
body, mind, and soul.*

Abundance flows in all areas of my life.

Adjustment

Day One

Fully experiencing your life means learning to adjust to its curves, twists, and nuances that are thrown at you on a daily basis. Every time you adjust, something else comes along to throw you out of your comfort zone, be it a mental, physical, or geographic one. How do you react? Do you go willingly, or do you fight it all the way? Today, think about making a visit to a chiropractor for an "adjustment." The physical adjustment can help ease your mental adjustment.

I easily adjust to all life experiences.

Day Two

Sometimes, when you think you have your life all mapped out, something happens that places you in a different direction. Perhaps you had in your mind the perfect mate, when you suddenly find yourself attracted to someone who does not fit that picture at all. Do you stay with "the plan" or do you start anew?

My expectations adjust to unexpected avenues of action.

Day Three

Maybe you love the town or city where you live, and you get transferred through your job, or an opportunity arises that means moving somewhere that never, ever entered your mind before. Perhaps you just purchased a house, or invested in a new pool. Your friends and family, may live here. Now you have to leave. How do you react to this news?

My mind-pattern adjusts to allow unrecognized opportunities to manifest.

Day Four

In the physical body, teeth hold the mind-pattern of adjustment. How are your teeth? Are you grinding them at night from resistance to adjustment? Do you need to visit a dentist but are delaying the visit? If you have not done so recently, make an appointment to have your teeth checked, cleaned, and repaired. If you need orthodontia work, but resist because of age or circumstance, consider this as well. Many adults have their teeth adjusted, and with new techniques it is barely noticeable to others.

Adjusting my physical body adjusts my mind-pattern.

Day Five

Perhaps you go to eat at your favorite restaurant only to find it no longer has your favorite item on the menu. Or, you think of the "perfect gift" for a close friend, but the store is out and cannot get it in time. How well do you adjust to the news? How many little irritations happen that, when combined, may be a way to redirect you toward another path?

My path in life adjusts with ease.

Day Six

Make a list of other things in your life that need adjusting, whether it is the brakes on your car or the frames of your glasses! Making adjustments in your outer life installs the mind-pattern of making adjustments in your inner life.

I adjust my outer life to correct my inner mind-pattern.

Day Seven

Holding onto stress and tension prevents people from adjusting, as well as creates the need to control and manipulate. Give all these emotions up to your Oversoul. Trust your Oversoul to guide and direct you in ways that the conscious mind has not yet imagined and comprehended.

My Oversoul adjusts my life in Divine Order.

I easily adjust to all life experiences.

Adversity

Day One

Adversity surrounds everyone. Adversity is designed to challenge and test you to the "nth" degree. Adversity may be large or small circumstances that create discomfort in some way. You may feel that your path is always bumpy because as soon as you think it is smooth, something happens to disrupt your life. Rather than become upset when adversity presents itself, embrace it for the new direction that it turns you toward. Think about the times when adversity pointed you in a new direction that ultimately was better for you.

I embrace all adversity in my life.

Day Two

The key to successfully facing adversity is to move through it, rather than fight or stay in it. In other words, what challenges can you move through yet still remain clean, clear, calm, and focused in your personal journey. Today, think about both personal and global adversity. How do you perceive it affects you?

I move through adversity with calm and focus.

Day Three

Many people spend a lot of time avoiding adversity. Usually the thought is worse than the experience. Without adversity, you would not be able to successfully explore the full spectrum of experience. If everything was always peaceful, most people would lose their motivation for movement, growth, and change. Sometimes it is necessary to take two or three steps backward to gain four or five steps forward.

Adversity brings forward movement.

Day Four

Adversity usually brings experiential learning, which is the best kind of learning process. This means that you actively incorporate all knowledge into yourself on many levels. You do not read from a book, or hear a story from someone else. You live and breathe life in a way that changes you forever.

Adversity teaches me experientially.

Day Five

Adversity often forces you into areas of yourself that you never realize existed. Adversity may force you to use up all your resources. After you use up your "known" resources, you get into the really creative parts of yourself that open and expand your horizons in ways you never before consciously thought about.

Adversity opens my creative resources.

Day Six

Adversity forces you to face your deepest fears. Rather than wait for adversity to bring these fears to your attention, proactively let your fears come to the surface now. Work though them on the Oversoul level so that you do not have to outpicture them in this reality. As long as you experience your fears, it does not matter where it happens. Facing your fears brings you into balance.

Adversity allows me to overcome my deepest fears.

Day Seven

Adversity is not your enemy. It is one of your greatest teachers, directing and focusing you in ways that you have not yet explored. Adversity is real life interactive drama that adds richness and flavor to all that you do. Adversity is not about peace, love, and light. It is about moving you into the explorations of the depths of God-Mind, nudging you onward and inward, even through your own reluctance. When adversity presents itself, know that you are strong and ready for the experiences that it brings.

I am ready for all experiences that adversity brings.

I move through adversity with calm and focus.

Alone

Day One

Whether you are in a room alone or with others, many people feel emotionally isolated. If this applies to you, then stop to think about the mind-pattern that creates this. Why do you attract people with whom you do not feel any emotional attachment? Or, do you have emotional attachment to them, but in a negative way?

I identify positive and negative emotional attachments.

Day Two

If you determine that you surround yourself with negative emotional attachments, then the next question to ask is, "Why?" Why do you position yourself in such a way that you are emotionally isolated? Do you have self-worth issues that say you only deserve to be alone?

I deserve to be surrounded by like-minded people.

Day Three

Are you alone because you do not want the responsibilities that come with emotional attachments? Emotional attachments mean that you now have others to consider. Regardless of who you think you want in your life—friend, companion, spouse, lover, child— time spent with him/her means less time for yourself. How do you feel about that?

I allow emotional attachment to others.

Day Four

Allowing others into your life means commitment. How do you feel about that? Relationships of any kind mean challenges, effort, and sometimes work. Relationships may mean that "when the going gets tough, the tough get going." The ride of life can be bumpy for one person. An additional person or two can complicate the ride as well as make it more enjoyable. Are all parts of you willing to take the negative along with the positive within a committed relationship?

I am willing to make commitments to others.

Day Five
No longer being alone means allowing yourself to be vulnerable. Anyone that is up close and personal sees the real you; the weaknesses as well as the strengths. Are you willing to allow others to see your weaknesses? Would you prefer to stay closed and alone to try to control who can and cannot cause any emotional hurt? Are you willing to be open and vulnerable?

I am willing to be open and vulnerable in my relationships.

Day Six
Perhaps fear keeps you alone. What if you develop relationships and then you cannot keep them? Is it better not to have any relationship at all so that you do not have to risk losing it? Do you deserve emotionally enriching relationships? Do you deserve to keep emotionally enriching relationships?

I deserve emotionally enriching relationships.

Day Seven
When you complain about being alone, or feel sorry for this aspect of your life, stop to think about what you give up when you bring someone else into your life. When there is a strong part of yourself that is unwilling to give up something to get something, then you will only sit and dream about "what if." When this happens, the dream is stronger than the reality that the smaller part of you wishes to create. When the desire to be with others is stronger than the desire to be alone, then that which you desire has no choice but to come to fruition. Think about this.

My desire to be with others is stronger than my desire to be alone.

I deserve emotionally enriching relationships.

Anchors

Day One

As you move forward with new plans and ideas, you sometimes find old habits and mind-patterns trying to pull you back. This can be disconcerting, as the greater percentage of you already functions in the new level. However, there may be a small percentage of you that is strong and resistant to going with the forward flow. It is important to address this small percentage so that you can bring all your energy together to fully function at your optimum level.

I release the need for old anchors that hold me back.

Day Two

Symbolically, look for anchors in your present that hold you to any part of your past that you no longer need. Even though you have cleaned and cleaned, there may be items that are hidden or stored that are no longer healthy for you. These could be old eyeglasses when you wear contact lenses, old letters from relationships that no longer exist, and/or mementos from unpleasant times. Search for the physical anchors that hold you into your old levels.

I identify old anchors that hold me back.

Day Three

Release these old anchors from your physical space. This represents releasing old anchors from your mental space. As these old anchors disperse, mentally ask your Oversoul to bless them and the experiences that they represent. Ask that the energy surrounding these anchors be returned to everyone via the involved Oversouls.

I release all anchors that I no longer need.

Day Four

Now think about what you can keep in your space to anchor you into your new level. Perhaps it is a book, a picture, a coin, an item of clothing. Create new anchors that hold you in the new level, symbolizing the mental anchors that hold your new mind-pattern in place.

I create new anchors to hold me in my new level of existence.

Day Five

Keep your focus on your new anchors. Whenever old mind-patterns start trying to reestablish themselves, take a look at this. Then, release everything up to your Oversoul, focusing on your new mental and physical anchors. Resist the urge to be pulled back into old mind-patterns.

My new anchors hold me in my new level of existence.

Day Six

Realize that as you continue to move forward, you continue to release physical items, symbolizing mental mind-patterns that no longer fit in your spiral of upward movement. This is an ongoing process as you continually evolve and refine yourself and your goals. Whatever you hold in your physical space, do so with meaningful awareness.

I release old anchors to make room for the new.

Day Seven

Realize that the further you move into your new mind-pattern, or your new level of existence, the more anchors you develop to hold you there. You move continually deeper into the mind-pattern with continually more anchors. One by one, you remove these anchors to replace them with new ones until you are at the door of a new level. Then, the process repeats itself as long as you allow it to do so.

I now have new anchors.

I release all anchors that I no longer need.

Anger

Day One

Anger takes many forms. You may live in a geographical area that reflects an anger mind-pattern. For example, do you live in an active volcano or earthquake-prone area? Is the Earth's expression and/or potential expression in your area a reflection of your own mind-pattern? What about the other people that live there? How would you assess their general temperaments?

I objectively observe the outer reflection of inner angers.

Day Two

Many people are full of anger, but do not even recognize that anger exists within. For example, do you get angry when you stub your toe, drop something and it breaks, other drivers get in your way, the paper is late, you lose something, the weather takes a turn for the worse, or the news reports something that you consider "bad" ? All these are subtle forms of anger that are creating within your body, mind, and soul. Observe when and how you express anger.

I objectively observe the anger within myself.

Day Three

Do you have an explosive temperament? Does it spiral out of control? Do you suppress your angers into your physical body, creating such physical issues as infections, boils, and fevers? Whenever anger is out of balance, there is an excess of red energy in your auric field. Release this storehouse of red anger energy out the top of your head to your Oversoul, watching it flow and flow. Remember, your Oversoul always stays clean. You can release this energy any time of the day or night, no matter what you are doing.

I release my excess red anger energy up to my Oversoul.

Day Four

Besides the physical body, take a look around your environment to see how your inner anger manifests in the outer world. This could be a dirty oven, a potential fire hazard such as a chimney or fireplace that needs to be cleaned out, a car that overheats, or accidents that release the anger energy out of your auric field. Whatever you find, make a decision about how you can clean the physical representation to help clean up your inner mind-pattern.

I release the outer manifestations of my inner angers.

Day Five

Whenever you feel angry, mentally place yourself in ice blue to cool yourself off, or surround yourself with brown for grounding. Breathe yourself into your center to control anger before it controls you.

I am in control of all my emotions.

Day Six

Remember, you are not getting rid of anger. Anger in its proper place is important. You may speak to someone that can only understand through anger, or at least the appearance of anger. Anger may be a motivator for self-change. When you are finally angry enough, you do something about whatever needs fixing! Observe anger in its proper place. As long as you are in control of anger, you can turn it on and off like a water faucet.

All my emotions are in balance.

Day Seven

Practice your anger releasing/balancing work today. Review your physical body to see where anger has improperly settled. Review your outer environment for the same purpose. Think of others that you may have harmed with your words. On the Oversoul level, ask forgiveness from these people for your words and actions. Finally, ask forgiveness for yourself.

My inner and outer worlds are in emotional balance; I am at peace.

I release my excess red anger energy up to my Oversoul.

Appreciation

Day One

There are many different directions that life can take. This means that it is easy to focus on what you do not have. This week, focus on what you do have. In order to move into anything newer, bigger, and better, start exactly where you are. You must appreciate all the learning and experiences that your life has brought. If you hate your life, the strength of that emotion keeps these types of experiences tied to you. Similarly, if you love something too much, the strength of that emotion ties the experiences to you. Appreciation brings balance as well as awareness of the positive and negative sides of every experience.

I appreciate all that I have and all that I receive.

Day Two

Look around your home. Think about all that is positive within your environment. How can you appreciate the little aggravations that you might see? Use your creative mind to turn the tables to learn something interesting about your growth experience.

I appreciate my home and surroundings.

Day Three

Review your relationships, including any that trouble you. Realize the learning that each brings. Appreciate whatever it is that you are learning from each relationship, regardless of the challenge.

I appreciate all my relationships.

Day Four

What kind of work are you involved in? Are you satisfied with what you do for a living? Are you interested in making drastic changes? Or minor changes? Or does the status quo suit you? Take any lemons that you see, and make yourself a cup of lemonade!

I appreciate my work.

Day Five

Using your mind's eye, take a look at your physical body. What is its state of health? What is it teaching you? Patience? Acceptance? Self-worth? Self-love?

I appreciate my physical body.

Day Six

What do you do well? Are you a great listener? A great conversationalist? Good at putting people at ease? An artist? A handyman? Computer expert? What are your finer qualities?

I appreciate myself and my abilities.

Day Seven

Think about all the people who would give anything to have what you have—your home, your relationships, your work, your body, your talents. Think about the less fortunate and those that would gladly trade your situation for their situation. Be grateful that "except for the grace of God, there go I."

I appreciate the world that I have created for myself.

I appreciate all that I have and all that I receive.

Avoidance

Day One
Sometimes you may be aware of your issues, but simply choose to avoid them. This may seem the easiest way to go for the moment. Look around your physical space to see if there are any physical tasks that you avoid. If so, do something today to complete this physical task.

I release the need to avoid my issues.

Day Two
There may be people in your life you choose to avoid for various reasons. Take some time today, on the Oversoul level, to internally discuss these particular issues.

I consciously stop my mind-pattern of avoidance.

Day Three
You may have some emotional issues that you have consciously buried because it seemed easiest at the time. Realize that when you stop running away from something, you are free to start running toward what you really want and desire in your life.

I tap into my inner resources to deal with all emotional issues.

Day Four
Do you avoid exploring your negative qualities because they make you uncomfortable? Are you now strong enough, and willing, to examine them? Take a look at the people in your life who annoy you with their irritating negative qualities. Anyone who creates a reaction within you is taking the time to teach you something about yourself. What is it?

I release the need to avoid the negative parts of Self.

Day Five

Do you avoid family issues? Perhaps there is someone with whom you need to speak? Or perhaps there is someone who you need to put in his/her place instead of vice versa? Holding these kinds of thoughts and feelings inside tears you down on all levels. Perhaps it is time that you cleared the air or set some boundaries. Are you now strong enough to face these issues? Do your Oversoul work. Make a decision to address these issues the next time the opportunity presents itself.

I release the need to avoid family issues.

Day Six

Do you avoid doing positive things for yourself? Is it time to work on your physical, emotional, mental, and/or spiritual needs. Have you allowed yourself the opportunity to do this? Take some time today to do just one thing for yourself but have not done. This does not have to be something major, but do start the energy flow toward positive self-enhancement.

I release the need to avoid positive self-enhancement.

Day Seven

Today, think about any other avoidance issues that you have. Realize that these are the issues that need your attention the most. They may be the most painful, traumatic, and/or uncomfortable, but they are your greatest propellers into your next level of awareness. These issues must be cleaned out so that they are never repeated again. Only you know what these issues truly are, and only you can deal with them.

*I release the need to avoid the experiences that are
my greatest teachers.*

I release the need to avoid the negative parts of Self.

Aura Cleaning

Day One

Most people carry extra weight in the aura because they do not take the time to clean this layer of Self. Cleaning your aura is extremely simple. You feel better, clearer, and your inner communication vastly improves. Today, quickly take a look around yourself. Notice how far out your aura extends. With your mind, pull your aura in close to your body. Put a bubble around it so that it is contained within a specific boundary. Keep this boundary around yourself today.

I am aware of the boundaries of my aura.

Day Two

After you pull in your aura so that it is close to your body, put a bubble around it. Inhale from the top of your head to the base of your spine. Exhale from the base of your spine out the top of your head, up to your Oversoul. Breathe yourself in and breathe yourself out. This pulls your aura inward, allowing you to feel centered and aligned along your spine.

I consciously pull myself into my center.

Day Three

With your eyes closed, observe what is inside your aura. Notice the colors, shapes, and consistency within your aura. Feel your breath create a vacuum along your spine as you breathe in and out. Breathe in violet for cleansing, then breathe out all within your aura that you no longer need. Watch what you no longer need flow and flow and flow out through the top of your head, and up into your Oversoul. As the "old" empties out, allow the bubble to remain filled with violet. Feel your aura become cleaner and clearer.

My breath is a cleansing tool.

Day Four

With your eyes closed, look inside your aura to see if you have any unnecessary cords attaching you to other people, places, and/or things. Ask your Oversoul to remove these attachments. Ask that this energy, which is yours, be returned to you via the involved Oversouls. Watch these attachments fall out of, and away from, everyone and everything involved, returning the energy up to your Oversoul. Let all the cords go.

I release all unnecessary attachments.

Day Five

With your eyes closed, look inside your aura to see if you have any unnecessary cords attaching other people, places, and/or things to you. Ask your Oversoul to remove these unnecessary attachments. Ask that the energy of the cords be returned to their rightful owners via the involved Oversouls. Watch these attachments fall out of, and away, from you. Let them go.

All unnecessary attachments are released from me.

Day Six

With your eyes closed, take a look inside your aura. Does it feel empty? If so, fill it with any color from your Oversoul that feels comfortable to you. You could choose violet for protection and healing, pink for unconditional love, blue for peace, or gold for wisdom, for example. Realize that when you empty out your aura of all the unnecessary "junk," it will feel empty. Take the time to fill your aura with something of your choosing so that you do not invite all the old junk back.

I fill my aura with positive growth and expansion.

Day Seven

Do you feel better since you took the time to clean your aura? Do you feel lighter and more energetic? Ask your Oversoul to provide a sign from the outer world to confirm your inner work. Give thanks when it happens.

The outer world confirms my inner work.

I consciously pull myself into my center.

Balance

Day One

With a hectic, chaotic lifestyle, it is easy for life to become unbalanced. Outer imbalances are reflections of inner imbalances. How balanced is your physical body? Can you stand on one foot only without holding onto anything? For how long? Can you put a sock on one foot while standing on the other? Can you raise your hands above your head while standing on one foot? Try these things, and think up some for yourself! A simple test of balance!

My physical body is in balance.

Day Two

Are your bank statements and checkbook in balance? The way you deal with your outer energy (money) represents how you deal with your inner energy. Take the time to keep your finances in an orderly fashion.

My inner and outer energies are in balance.

Day Three

Are your left-brain and right-brain in balance? Walking is a great way to connect the two—left foot, right foot, left foot, right foot. Allow your arms to hang and swing freely at your sides, unencumbered by packages, briefcases, and/or purses. Walk your way into inner balance.

My left-brain and right-brain are in balance.

Day Four

Are your emotions in balance? How is your anger, frustration, and stress level? Do you blow up at the drop of a hat? Are you tightly wound like a clock? You do not want to eliminate these qualities from your personal recipe, but you do not want them to have more importance than necessary. Breathe your excess red energy out the top of your head, up into your Oversoul until you see only pale red energy—just the right amount to keep yourself in balance.

All my negative emotions are in perfect balance.

Day Five

Are your love and compassion emotions in balance? Do you run them, or do they run you? Do you love someone so much that you manipulate and control him/her into doing "the right thing" according to you? Do you love food, alcohol, shopping, etc. so much that you allow them to control you? Does compassion for the world's perceived injustices overwhelm you, leaving you with guilt that you cannot do more? As with all things, love and compassion can become out of balance. Release all the excess deep pink energy out of your aura by breathing it out the top of your head up to your Oversoul until it becomes a pale pink.

All my positive emotions are in perfect balance.

Day Six

The past, present, and future, are only linear illusions. Yet, sometimes people allow these timeframes to get out of balance. Some people focus on the past, never leaving it. Some people cannot deal with the past or the future, so they ignore it all and focus solely on the present. Some people live in the future to avoid the present and the past. Are your past, present, and future in balance? Have you explored your past enough to learn from it and let it go? Are you dealing with your present, even the unpleasantness? Are you consciously creating your future now?

My past, present, and future are in perfect balance.

Day Seven

Do you spend more time on your outer quest than you do on your inner one? How many books do you have, seminars do you attend, videos do you watch, music do you listen to? Are your outer pursuits in harmony with one another, or are they chaotic diversions of your time and talents? Whatever you do, integrate all activities to focus and achieve inner and outer balance. Discard all but the core of your outer quest, spending equal quality time on the inner quest.

My inner quest for Self, Oversoul, and God-Mind is in balance.

My inner and outer energies are in balance.

Best

Day One
Many people have experienced the worst that this reality has to offer. Now it is time to assimilate that experience so you can move into experiencing the best that this reality has to offer. Making this transition can be difficult, as the negative is a wonderful teacher. Even with the pain and trauma that it has brought, most people have difficulty making that leap of consciousness into accepting the positive side of this reality.

I accept and allow the best that this reality offers.

Day Two
Once you agree to accept the best, self-sabotage routines may kick in, preventing you from attaining your goal. Have you ever been on the precipice of something really great, but you could not make the leap to bring it to you? Or, have you had really great opportunities that you have "blown"? Are you done with this kind of mind-pattern?

I deserve the best that this reality offers.

Day Three
What kind of relationships do you have in your life? Are you satisfied with them? Could they be better? Do you have the best relationships that this reality has to offer? Do you deserve to have the best? What mind-pattern will bring the best relationships to you?

I have the best relationships that this reality offers.

Day Four

Do you have the best physical, mental, and emotional health that is possible in this reality? Do you even have any idea of what that might be? Is it possible to be healthier beyond your most vivid dreams? With the strength of your mind-pattern, bring this to you.

I have the best health possible to attain in this reality.

Day Five

Are you happy with your financial status? Could it be better? What is your mind-pattern that brings your income stream to you?

I have the best income stream that this reality offers.

Day Six

Are you looking for secret knowledge in this reality? Are you continually seeking deeper, more in-depth answers? What is the mind-pattern that brings this knowledge to you?

I have the best knowledge that this reality offers..

Day Seven

What mind-pattern prevents you from attaining the best at whatever you do? Are you ready to release it? Are you done with self-sabotage routines? Are you ready to accept the positive as your greatest teacher? What mind-pattern can you develop to pull the best to you?

I am the best at whatever I choose to do.

I deserve the best that this reality offers.

Birth Family

Day One

Your original birth family is a reflection of your original goals for incarnating in this lifeline. These people represent what you need to experience as well as what mind-patterns need to be balanced and corrected. When reflecting back on your original birth family, do you believe that you know what each person within it represents for you, personally?

I understand my original purpose as reflected by my birth family.

Day Two

Have you spent a lifetime running away from your family, either emotionally or physically? If so, is it time to re-evaluate the meaning of each specific person within your family, as well as the interpersonal relationships that you observed while living with your family?

I understand why I chose my birth family.

Day Three

What did your birth family teach you about yourself? What do they still teach you? Do you like being with them, or do you avoid them? Why? Do they elevate you, hold you back, or help you maintain the status quo? Are you moving through the lessons that you agreed to learn pre-birth?

I review the lessons learned from my birth family.

Day Four

Are you able to view your birth family from an objective/Oversoul perspective? Do you see them as they are, rather than as you wish them to be? Are you able to accept them as they are? Do you judge them for what they are not? Do you see that they are different people now than at the time you lived with them? Did they change for the better, worst, or do they maintain the status quo?

I objectively evaluate my birth family.

Day Five

Does your birth family know which "buttons" to push? How do you react when they "push your buttons"? Do they have emotional control over you? If so, how do you allow this? Are there established behavior patterns that you need to consciously break? Have you discussed these patterns with them on the Oversoul level?

I accept only healthy behavior from my birth family.

Day Six

Are you able to view your birth family with compassion and understanding? If so, this is the first step to complete the correction of your own mind-pattern. When you understand them, you understand yourself. When you have compassion for them, you have compassion for yourself. They are only a reflection of what exists within you.

I view my birth family with compassion and understanding.

Day Seven

Does your birth family reflect your past, present, or future? Does this frighten or excite you? If they are your past, thank them for helping you get through that part of your life. If they are your present or future, decide if this is what you are willing to accept. Always remember that these people were the closest reflections of your mind-pattern when you were conceived. Rather than look away, search deeper to unlock truths to your own reason for existence in this reality.

My birth family teaches me about my original mind-patterns.

I understand why I chose my birth family.

Blackouts

Day One

Blackouts literally mean not being aware of what is going on around you. Are there areas in your life to which you need to pay more attention? Could there be events being set in motion to which you need to open your eyes? What kind of "personal" blackout is occurring in your life today?

I release the need for personal blackouts.

Day Two

Do the blackouts that randomly occur worldwide serve to trigger your own personal blackout? In other words, does your personal awareness shut down in response to news reports of blackouts?

I remain unaffected by outer world blackout events.

Day Three

If something exists in your world, then there is a part of you that contributes to it. What part of your life would you rather not see? What part of your life would you like to "black out?"

I release the need to black out any part of my life.

Day Four

Proactively work to resolve all circumstances that you want to black out. Release all that you no longer need so that you can progress forward.

I proactively resolve issues rather than black them out.

Day Five

Are you prepared for blackouts in your area? Do you have canned/dried food, bottled water, flashlights, batteries, extra cash on hand, a small first aid kit, and enough fuel in your car? Realize that these items of preparedness are reflections of your personal mind-pattern and your internal state of preparedness for mental blackouts. Prepare your outer world to prepare your inner world. Once prepared on all levels, release the need for such events in your life.

   I prepare my physical home to break the cycle of mental blackouts.

Day Six

Are you having a power grid failure in your life? Do you feel like your personal power source is failing you? Now is the time to pro-actively connect Self to Oversoul and God-Mind so that you are always connected to your source regardless of the circumstances of the outer world.

   I connect to my personal power grid to prevent personal blackouts.

Day Seven

Keep Self consciously connected twenty-four hours a day, seven days a week to your personal power Source: Oversoul and God-Mind. Keep the power flowing, recognizing that your personal power conduit is always active. The outer world only reflects that which already exists within. When you no longer have internal blackouts, there will no longer be external blackouts.

   My personal power grid illuminates my life.

I release the need for personal blackouts.

Blocking Triggers

Day One

You may feel triggered as a result of increased ELF and personal deprogramming work. Feelings of being triggered range from short tempers to suicide. Many people feel jittery, nervous, and constantly on edge, as if "something" is about to happen. Be aware of your reactions to both internal and external stimuli so that you can be in control of it instead of vice versa. Be vigilant in keeping your T-Bar archetype balanced and spinning your chakras to help center and calm yourself regardless of any circumstance.

I balance my T-Bar archetype and spin my chakras to block triggers.

Day Two

Keep the brown merger archetype at your pineal gland on a background of royal blue every second of every day and night. Keep a template under your pillow while sleeping and one on your body facing toward you for an extra boost. Spend some time drawing the brown merger archetype, or tracing it with your finger if necessary. Mentally place any known triggers on top of the brown merger archetype. This allows the trigger to merge with your personality so that you control it, rather than allowing it to control you.

I use the brown merger archetype to block triggers.

Day Three

The silver infinity archetype represents your connection to your Angelic frequency and Oversoul. When you feel especially depressed or in despair, this archetype pulls you up to your Oversoul level. Use the silver infinity archetype as necessary in all chakra bands as well as above your head. In addition, surround yourself and your surroundings in heavy violet.

The silver infinity archetype elevates me beyond all triggers.

Day Four

Sea salt helps to counter the effects of ELF and ground the physical body. Put a few tablespoons in your bath. Set small bowls around your house. A small bowl under your bed can aid your protection techniques during the night. A light sprinkle of sea salt on your food helps to stabilize the physical body.

The frequency of sea salt blocks all internal and external triggers.

Day Five

Use tones to shatter the parts of yourself that accept and allow internal and external triggers. Create tones to put everything back together in a new way that does not allow any trigger to penetrate the mind-pattern.

Tones block any trigger from affecting my mind-pattern.

Day Six

When you feel like you are responding to triggers of any kind, use food to pull yourself into your body. Eat heavy meats, starches, and grains to ground you into the body. Mentally surround yourself with the color "brown" for grounding.

I surround myself with brown and eat grounding food to block triggers.

Day Seven

Whether you are specifically programmed or programmed as part of the group mind, continually do your release work. The only way a trigger can affect you is if there is some part of you that allows it in. Look for holes and vulnerabilities within your own mind-pattern so that you can correct these before someone else finds them and uses them against you. This is already happening. You are the only one that can correct it.

I release all trigger-accepting mind-patterns.

I use the brown merger archetype to block triggers.

Blocks

Day One
Do you feel like you have blocks that keep you from accomplishing your goals? Look around your environment to see what kind of physical "blocks" surround you. Is your space free-flowing, or are there obstacles that are difficult for you to navigate around? Are your decorations full of "blocks"? Look for the physical symbols that "box" you in and keep you from reaching your goals. Change the flow of your physical environment to pave the way for the release of your inner blocks.

I change the flow of my physical environment to release inner blocks.

Day Two
What kind of blocks do you set up so that you cannot accomplish your goals? Do you have goals that you have worked on for years without success? Do your words say one thing but your actions say another? Or, do you feel one way inside, but express something different to the outer world? In what ways do you block your goals from reaching you?

I identify all blocks to my goals.

Day Three
Do you perceive that others block the way to your goals? Do you think thoughts such as, "If only he/she were gone, I would have what I want?" Do you realize that these people are only reflections of yourself? Until you understand what others reflect back, these people will stay in your life. Even if they do move on, you will pull similar people into your life or maybe worse, until your mind-pattern changes. You are the only one who holds these perceived "goal-blockers" in your life. Greet them as an opportunity for growth.

I release all people who I perceive as goal-blockers.

Day Four

Do you think that your finances block you from accomplishing your goals? Do you think thoughts such as, "If I only had the money, I would..." Open your mind to allow you to accomplish your goals. Work with your Oversoul to determine if your goals are in alignment with your highest good. Adjust your goals if necessary, but open to the reality of financial limitlessness.

I release all financial blocks up to my Oversoul.

Day Five

Do you have physical/health issues that prevent you from reaching your goals? Do you think that this means you should adjust your goals, or does this mean it is time to open your mind to physical healing? Is there some part of you that enjoys your physical/health issues...extra attention, needing to hear people say they love and/or care for you, or developing the mind over the body, as examples? Work with your Oversoul to determine how to proceed from an objective viewpoint.

I re-evaluate my physical issues to release blocks.

Day Six

How do you reinforce your blocks? Do your words hold you in place? Do you "doodle" little boxes or symbolically confining symbols? Do you invite "goal-blocking" people into your life and then are miserable when they are there? What can you do differently so that your blocks are not reinforced? Are you ready to change old ways to accomplish your goals?

I release all my block-reinforcement activities.

Day Seven

Do you ask for help from your Oversoul, but then do not accept the help that it gives? Do you recognize available help or because it comes in ways other than anticipated, you simply think that your Oversoul is ignoring you? Instead of determining how your Oversoul will help you, allow it to help you in the best way possible.

Help from my Oversoul allows me to easily move through all blocks.

I identify all blocks to my goals.

Body Systems

Day One

Every system of the physical body has a specific color when it is healthy. Work on keeping the correct color in the correct body area. Once the color is in place and you say your affirmation, ground everything in brown to anchor the color into the present. Always keep your legs and feet in brown to keep yourself anchored to the Earth. Focus on keeping pale red in the root chakra band to keep it balanced, level out your energy levels, and promote creativity.

I am energetic and creative.

Day Two

Pale orange in the next chakra band helps you to speak honestly, as well as determine the honesty of others. Keep yourself in pale orange when you speak. Place others in pale orange when they speak. This allows you to determine their motives.

I give and receive truth and honesty.

Day Three

Keep pale yellow in the digestive chakra band to promote internal health. If you have any digestive issues, determine what is in your life that you are not easily digesting and assimilating.

I easily digest and assimilate all of life's experiences.

Day Four

Medium green in the chest chakra band oxygenates the blood stream and allows for emotional healing. Keep these colors in and around you so that emotional issues can be resolved and released.

I am emotionally healthy.

Day Five

Ice blue in the throat and mouth chakra band aids your communication efforts. If you have any health issues here, always keep these areas in ice blue. Learn to tactfully speak up for yourself. Whatever you suppress creates negatively within your body systems.

I easily and effectively communicate.

Day Six

Keeping royal blue from the tip of your nose to the top of your head promotes vision, hearing, olfactory, and brain health and function. Royal blue helps colds, ear infections, eye problems, focus, and concentration.

My senses and brain all function at 100% capacity.

Day Seven

Keep violet at the top of the head to promote protection and conscious connection to your Oversoul and God-Mind.

I am consciously connected to my Oversoul and God-Mind.

I easily digest and assimilate all of life's experiences.

Boundaries

Day One

Where do you start and where do you stop? Take a moment to see how far out your aura extends. Using your mind, will your aura in closer to your body, and put a bubble around it. Now, you know where you start and where you stop.

I create clear boundaries of where I start and where I stop.

Day Two

On some level, others see that you are setting boundaries. This may mean that they will try to push you more. Often times, when you do the exact thing that you need, your life suddenly appears in turmoil or upheaval. This is because the new boundaries are tested by those around you. They do not like new rules to learn. They would prefer to push you back into familiar ground so they know how to react.

I move through the new challenges that new boundaries create.

Day Three

Are there people encroaching upon your boundaries? If so, this means that somewhere you are encroaching upon the boundaries of others. Take a few moments to determine where this might be. Look from the Oversoul level, as this may be in some subtle ways of which you are not consciously aware. Ask your Oversoul to direct you so that you can stop perpetuating old behaviors.

I identify where I encroach upon the boundaries of others.

Day Four

Setting physical boundaries helps to establish mental and emotional boundaries. Do you have physical boundaries that encroach upon the boundaries of others? For example, are all of your possessions in your own space, or do you have some of them in the work or home space of others? Do you respect the physical space of others? Bringing your physical possessions back into your space signifies bringing your mental/emotional possessions back within the boundaries of your own aura.

I establish physical boundaries to enforce mental/
emotional boundaries.

Day Five

Do others have physical possessions in your space? If so, return them as a way of saying that boundary encroachment is no longer tolerated. The possessions that you "borrow" hold the energy of others in your space. Do not allow or invite others to encroach upon your boundaries.

I am aware of when I invite others to encroach upon my boundaries.

Day Six

Setting and enforcing boundaries means that you become stronger without the distractions of others to defocus you. Your aura is clearer and cleaner, which means that your mind is clearer and cleaner. Working through the discomfort of changing the rules brings you greater inner focus and direction.

My boundaries provide inner clarity, focus, and direction.

Day Seven

As you establish your own boundaries, you will see others that need help establishing theirs. Remember not to judge them, even if they do not want your help. Work on the Oversoul level to instruct them so that when the time is ready, everything is in place for them to learn the lessons that you just walked through.

I teach others about establishing boundaries
via the Oversoul level.

I create clear boundaries of where I start & where I stop.

Career

Day One

If you are unhappy in your career, whatever form that takes, recognize that those feelings spill over into the workplace. This does not add to or uplift anyone, yourself included. In addition, your unhappiness could be the key that holds you where you no longer belong.

I greet my workday joyously.

Day Two

No matter what your career, there most likely is someone somewhere that would be grateful for the opportunity that you have. Appreciate what you have, focusing on the positives rather than the negatives.

I give thanks for my position at work.

Day Three

If you are ready to leave or advance, clean up your past so that you can move into your future.

I ask that my position be blessed on the Oversoul level,
and made ready for the next person.

Day Four

Recognize that before you can move into something else, you must be ready. In addition, all the other players must also be ready.

I am ready for the next opportunity, and the next
opportunity is ready for me.

Day Five

Perhaps you have a hidden fear of change. Perhaps this prevents your career moving into something different. Perhaps there is a part of you that would rather remain in the status quo rather than face an uncertain future.

I greet the challenge of a new career.

Day Six

Sometimes it feels safer to stay with what you know rather than embark on an unknown journey, even one with positive potentials. Do some different, fun things to get yourself "unstuck." Drive to work a different way, park in a different spot, eat a new kind of sandwich for lunch, and go to a different restaurant. Reach out to expand your horizons in some small way that imprints your consciousness with an entirely new way of approaching movement and growth.

I create pathways to a new, improved, fulfilling career.

Day Seven

Stop trying to force things to happen. Putting too much effort into something has the opposite effect; it be comes stifling and limit-ing. Do your mental work. Sit back and allow the energy to move you. Stop trying to force the energy to move.

I easily move into a fulfilling career.

I greet the challenge of a new career.

Change

Day One

Hold your arms above your head. Bend and sway from side to side. Next, bend over with your hands toward the floor. Do not try to touch the floor. Simply hang. Stand up, arms outstretched from your sides. With arms extended, twist left to right, then right to left. Repeat the following affirmation as you move your physical body.

I am flexible.

Day Two

Change your morning routine. For example, if you normally brush your teeth first, brush them last. If you normally put your shirt on first and then your pants, reverse the order. If you always have toast and coffee, have cereal and juice. If you never eat breakfast, have something; if you always eat breakfast, skip it.

I am willing to change.

Day Three

Change your evening routine. For example, if you always read before going to bed, listen to music instead. If you have a cup of tea, have a glass of warm apple juice with cinnamon. Go to bed a half-hour later or earlier. Sleep on the "other" side of the bed.

I enjoy the challenge of change.

Day Four

Wear your watch on the "other" arm. Eat with your "other" hand. Drink your morning coffee from a different cup. Drive to work using a different route. Park in a different parking spot. Start your shopping from the "other" side of the store.

I am comfortable in the midst of my discomfort.

Day Five

Change your daily routine. Anything that breaks up your regular routine forces you to think differently. Unused brain cells are stimulated into action. Creative thinking sets the stage for change.

I reconfigure the neuro-network of my brain.

Day Six

Make a list of challenges (people, places, things, situations, relationships, etc.) that bother you. Prioritize them from the most challenging to the least challenging. Release the list up to your Oversoul; let it go.

New solutions to old situations now come forth.

Day Six

Review yesterday's list. Choose one challenge. Begin to resolve it by using a different approach than ever before. Know that new actions mean new resolutions.

I accept and implement the new.

I am willing to change.

Childhood Issues

Day One

Most of what you do today is a result of your early, formative, childhood years. Whatever you experienced at that time, you recreate in a variety of forms so that you can "work it out." Over and over again, you set up the same scenario with different people. Review your life to determine what scenarios you continually recreate—both positive and negative.

I easily determine repetitive scenarios in my life.

Day Two

Most of these experiences happened under the age of five. Surround yourself in dark green, representing your emotional past. Visualize a dark green spiral staircase, representing your DNA. Move your consciousness down the staircase until you come to a pale orange door labeled "Under Age 5." Go through the door to examine this period of your life. If you feel trauma of any kind, surround yourself in brown. Stop the visualization.

I objectively review my life under the age of five.

Day Three

Repeat the visualization from yesterday. Remain in your center as you review this time period of your life. Specifically, observe your childhood primary caregivers. These are the people who most closely reflected your own mind-pattern at that particular point in time. Why did you attract them into your life? What did/do you need to learn in this life from them? Are they still teaching you?

I understand the initial mind-pattern that brought me to this planet.

Day Four

Have you dealt with your leftover feelings from this period in your life? Do you understand your life from both logical and emotional viewpoints?

I reconcile my life before the age of five.

Day Five

Once you open up long-sealed memories, release the energy that holds them within you. This energy has weight, color, tone, and consistency. Release this energy out through the top of your head, up into your Oversoul. Whatever you feel, allow it to go. Remain in your center, while your emotional side expresses on the Oversoul level. Your Oversoul relays the message to any other involved Oversouls. Do not hold anything back.

I release emotional attachment to my life before the age of five.

Day Six

Childhood experiences need to move out of you to continue the upward evolutionary spiral of your soul-personality. Release anything that you are recreating up to your Oversoul. You can work your issues out on a mental level. You no longer need to experience them in physical reality.

I release the need to recreate my childhood.

Day Seven

Whenever you remove something, you must replace it with something else. Fill the voids from all your releasing work with the color of medium green to fill the void as well as create emotional healing.

I fill all voids within with medium green for emotional healing.

I release the need to recreate my childhood.

Choices

Day One

All the choices that you make set events in motion. Think about how many choices you make every day simply out of habit. These are the choices that you never stop to think about. Look at your choices to determine if these are still the best choices at this time in your life. These choices might vary from how you get up in the morning to what you choose to eat to how you drive your car to how you spend your day.

I consciously evaluate my daily choices.

Day Two

Every choice that you make sets the events in motion for the next event. You have a multiple choice "test" in front of you every second of every day, with multiple options. Your choice determines what occurs next. When you evaluate your options, carefully think about the long-term outcomes of your short-term decisions. Do you need to make different choices or is your pathway moving along in a satisfactory way?

I evaluate the long-term outcomes of my choices.

Day Three

What past choices have you made with negative outcomes? Did you learn from those choices, or do you continue to repeat them?

I evaluate my negative choices.

Day Four

What past choices have you made with positive outcomes? Did you learn from those choices? Do you know how to repeat these kinds of choices at will to enhance positive outcomes?

I evaluate my positive choices.

Day Five

Sometimes people make choices just to affect some kind of change or movement, not really caring if the outcome is positive or negative. Have you ever made these kinds of choices? Was it worth the risk you took? Would you do it again? If so, is there any situation in your current life to which this type of choice is applicable?

I make appropriate choices to affect immediate change.

Day Six

Sometimes people are not even aware that they have choices because they are so locked into specific behavior patterns. Have you uncovered any area where you finally realize that you do have a choice? If so, what have you chosen to do with this information?

I always have a choice.

Day Seven

Have you ever blamed anyone else for a choice that you made? Regardless of input from others, all choices are ultimately yours; you are ultimately responsible. Learn from these choices. It is possible to listen to others, but always give the information up to your Oversoul to find out if this advice is applicable to your situation or not. Ask your Oversoul and God-Mind for guidance. Be willing to accept the responsibility for the outcome of your choice, whatever that may be.

I always make the wisest choice.

I always have a choice.

Clarity

Day One

Sometimes when you are between levels of awareness, it is difficult to sort the different layers to determine what belongs to the past, present, and the future that is in process. You are like a big jellyfish, working to bring all parts of Self through one door. Yet, not all parts of Self willingly line up at the gate to go. Some want to remain in the past, some want to stay in the present, and some already exist in the future. Start the mental sorting process today.

I see my past, present, and future with clarity.

Day Two

You may feel like you are diligently working without any results. This is because you are working on many parts of yourself at one time. One part shifts a little, and then another part shifts, and so forth. Does your entire life look and feel like a juggling act? Is it time to eliminate activities or downsize responsibilities? If so, what can go and what can stay?

I review my activities with clarity.

Day Three

Take a look at your environment to see what you hold onto that does not need to be in your present moment. Perhaps this might be your motivation for a garage sale, or to donate to charity or the nearest garbage can!

I see my path with clarity.

Day Four

Clean your windows, mirrors, television screen, computer screen, video camera, and sunglasses—anything that you can think of that is connected with seeing clearly.

I focus with clarity.

Day Five

Pick up any book or newspaper. Flip through the pages, allowing your eyes to glance at words or paragraphs. Allow yourself to choose the appropriate places to stop for a few seconds. What are the words really saying and why? Allow yourself to sort useful information from the rubbish.

I read with clarity.

Day Six

As you listen to others, clarify why you are listening—because you want to, because you have invested so much time and energy that you feel you should, because others say you should?

I listen with clarity.

Day Seven

Why do you say the words that you speak? Do you know what you want to convey? Do you say "I'm hungry" but what you mean is, "I'm bored"? Do you say "I'm angry" but what you mean is, "I've had a hard day"? What message do you want to convey?

I speak with clarity.

I see my past, present, and future with clarity.

Cleansing

Day One

In preparation for cleansing, it is important to satiate and fulfill as many desires as possible so that they do not creep up on you later. You can do this either on a mental or physical level. Physically, do what you need to do to complete and fulfill your desires. Or, you can mentally visualize the completion and fulfillment of your desires.

I prepare for personal cleansing.

Day Two

Use today to complete your physical and/or mental desires that you prefer not to carry forward into the next phase of your life. For example, you may want to eat a plate of cookies, or lounge around all day long doing absolutely nothing. Bring these kinds of desires to conclusion by fulfilling them before you begin your cleanse. This allows you to successfully cleanse without personal restrictions.

I successfully cleanse without personal restrictions.

Day Three

Feel the thrust of the cleanse propelling you forward into your goals. Feel the weight of the old falling away from all levels of your being. Observe the old weight moving out through the top of your head, up to your Oversoul.

I feel the cleanse propelling me forward.

Day Four

Use a tablespoon of fresh lemon juice in distilled water to help break up the past that is holding on like glue in your physical body. This is a result of mind-patterns that are cemented in and are ready for removal—usually fear-based. Continue this daily for as long as you feel necessary.

I cleanse old, fear-based mind-patterns from all levels of my being.

Day Five

Your skin is your largest organ of elimination. If possible, take a nice long bath using Epsom salts, mustard powder, baking soda, or sea salt to pull toxins from your body. This represents release of toxic mind-patterns. Continue this routine for as long as you feel necessary.

I cleanse toxic mind-patterns from all levels of my being.

Day Six

If your toothpaste contains fluoride, you might want to consider replacing it with one that does not. You may consider using baking soda. Fluoride was originally conceived during WWII in the Nazi concentration camps as a way to dull the minds and make people more controllable. Check your vitamins for fluoride as well.

My cleansed mind is quick and alert.

Day Seven

Reduce the amount of preservatives and artificial sweeteners as much as possible. These slow down the flow of psychic, or personal, energy throughout your body. Your psychic energy is the energy necessary for proper functioning of the body, such as digestion, breathing, and walking.

I cleanse my psychic energy flow.

I feel the cleanse propelling me forward.

Clear Path

Day One

There is now, and always has been, much upheaval in the world. Even as you read this, there is a part of you that is going through this in other lifelines. Staying clear and focused regardless of outer world activities is always your goal. How rough can the outer world become while you walk focused and clear on your chosen path?

I walk focused and steadfast on my clear path.

Day Two

How clean can you stay in how much dirt? How much controversy and adversity can you see all around yourself without partaking in it? If others choose to "get dirty," do you have to follow their lead? Who wins, who loses?

I remain clean on my clear path.

Day Three

Do you accept challenges or run from them? Do you isolate yourself from controversy and adversity, or do you greet the challenge? This does not mean put yourself in the path of a moving bus, but if something is definitely an issue, then you definitely need to face it—no matter how small, no matter how big. You cannot run from yourself—which is where all challenges originate.

I accept all challenges to effectively clear my path.

Day Four

Do you feed cycles and participate in them, or do you extricate yourself from them? What goes out must come back—this is how cycles perpetuate themselves. What cycles are you caught in? How can you extricate yourself? The deeper the cycle is ingrained, the more diligence needed to dig your way out. You built the cycle, now it is up to you to dismantle it.

My path is now clear of all non-serving cycles.

Day Five

Can you feel the energy of the collective conscious/unconscious without being affected by it? Do you feel nervous and jittery simply because others do? Do you react to manipulations of the group mind? Do your aura colors change to match others or do you keep your colors clean and clear?

I clearly see and walk my path through the density of the group mind.

Day Six

Visualize yourself as an ice-cutter ship. Extend your arms out in front, fingers extended with each hand touching the other. Visualize the energy of the outer world as you observe yourself cutting right through it all. In your center, align Self, Oversoul, and God-Mind. Feel the strength of this trinity as your focus effectively clears your path.

My focus effectively clears a path through the outer world.

Day Seven

Can your path be easy through such difficult times? What do you want it to be? What is the strength of your focus? Is it strong enough to pull an easy path to you? Is this what your soul-personality and Oversoul want for you? Do you release your fears up to your Oversoul as they arise? What is your mind-pattern building for you right now?

I easily create a clear path in every situation.

My path is now clear of all non-serving cycles.

Co-Creators

Day One
The reason that you exist in this physical reality is because the strength of your mind-pattern helps to co-create this existence. This physical reality merely reflects your mind-pattern back to you. This physical reality only exists because everyone agrees that it exists. If everyone suddenly pulled their energy out of this physical reality, it would effectively cease to exist. This applies to any circumstance in your life.
I am responsible for co-creating this physical reality.

Day Two
If global conflict exists, then there is a corresponding mind-pattern within you. What part of you specifically adds to the existing global conflict? Global conflict cannot exist in your world unless there is global conflict within you somewhere. What kind of "global," or overall, conflict exists within your mind-pattern?
I create global peace within to co-create global peace without.

Day Three
Do you disagree with the current political structure that exists in your outer world, however you may define that? If so, what are you doing to create political conflict within yourself? Do you agree with your own inner politics and organization?
My positive internal political organization co-creates positive external political organization.

Day Four
Does world poverty concern you? If so, then what part of you exists in poverty? Is it emotional, mental, spiritual, nutritional, and/or financial?
My internal abundance co-creates external abundance.

Day Five

What part of you co-creates the religions of the world? How does each one reflect your own mind-pattern? Do you judge and criticize them for perceived failures? Do you find them too controlling and contrived? What part of your belief system fails you, or is controlling and contrived?

My internal spiritual harmony co-creates external spiritual harmony.

Day Six

Do you disagree with the external educational system? If so, how do you educate yourself? How can you more effectively change your own internal educational process? What part of your mind-pattern needs to be educated in a different way?

My internal educational opportunities co-create external educational opportunities.

Day Seven

Do you have concern about the environment? What part of your internal environment is reflected in the external one? Do you have inner pollution that needs to be cleaned up? How about wasted or overused resources? Resources that are used up without replenishment?

My internal environmental harmony co-creates external environmental harmony.

I am responsibe for co-creating this physical reality.

Collective Mind-Pattern

Day One

Whatever you see in the outer world is simply an outpicturing of your inner world. It is the collective mind-pattern that creates all outer world circumstances. What is in your mind-pattern that adds to the collective mind-pattern? What would you prefer not to see in the outer world? For instance, if you prefer not to see starvation, where in your mind-pattern are you starving yourself and to what degree?

I acknowledge my addition to the collective mind-pattern.

Day Two

Do the outer world circumstances invoke feelings of fear, panic, or sometimes paranoia within you? If so, this is an opportunity for you to face these emotions. Choose something in your life that creates small fears in you. Are you afraid of being late, not having enough time, of being wrong, or not finding a parking space? Facing small aspects of fear helps you loosen the grip of fear.

I face my fear to help the collective mind-pattern.

Day Three

Refuse to participate in some behavior that you know is not correct, such as an argument, ridiculing someone, or gossiping. All these little "incorrect" behaviors add to the world's collective mind-pattern.

I add only correct behavior to the collective mind-pattern.

Day Four

Do you have any unresolved inner conflicts that add to the out-picturing of collective conflicts? Should you stay where you are or move? Change jobs or stay where you are? Buy new clothes or keep the old ones? Inner conflict occurs every day. Some you hold onto longer than others. The collective mind-pattern simply outpictures what occurs within every person. Resolving your own inner conflicts adds this knowledge to the collective mind-pattern.

I resolve inner conflicts to help the collective mind-pattern.

Day Five

Do you have excess ego out of balance? Do you allow others to tell you who and what you are? Do you agree to their definition of what you should/should not be or do you set your own standards? Do you see excess ego in political, industry, and entertainment leaders? Is this a reflection of you and if so where? Can changing your own ego when it is out of balance change the outpicturing of world events?

I balance my ego to help the collective mind-pattern.

Day Six

Do you lie about how you feel, what you do/do not want, or to protect others? These "little lies" feed the collective mind-pattern, taking away its ability to outpicture the truth. Think about what you say and why. Work on aligning Self, Oversoul, and God-Mind, with feelings, thoughts, and words to bring forth the truth at all times.

I bring forth my own truth to help the collective mind-pattern.

Day Seven

Continue to identify what you add to the collective mind-pattern, both positive and negative. Make conscious choices about what you do and how it affects not only yourself and immediate environment, but also how it affects the world collective mind-pattern.

I carefully choose what I add to the collective mind-pattern.

I face my fear to help the collective mind-pattern.

Collective Unconscious

Day One

Every thought you think not only affects your entire system within and without, but it also joins with the collective unconscious of humanity. Each thought that flows from you automatically imprints the collective unconscious. What kind of an imprint would you like to put into place?

I carefully consider my imprint upon the collective unconscious.

Day Two

What are you imprinting upon it now? Think about your general thoughts. What kind of "themes" emit from you? Struggle, hopelessness, despair, lack, appreciation, thankfulness, Self/Oversoul/God-Mind communication? Around what "themes" does your collective unconscious imprinting revolve?

*I identify the main themes with which I imprint the
collective unconscious.*

Day Three

Are you creating a trail for others of upward movement? If you struggle, do you eventually make progress? Do you work on your mind-pattern of ease? Could others grasp the concept of ease, or do you think they need some additional rungs on the ladder before they can move with ease? Are you following the imprint of others?

*I create a trail of upward movement within the
collective unconscious.*

Day Four

Do you think that making a change within yourself allows for others to make similar changes? For example, when you stand up for yourself, do you think this paves the way for others to stand up for themselves?

My inner changes create a blueprint within the collective unconscious.

Day Five

Do you pull the collective unconscious up or down? Does it pull you up or down? Who is in control? Who do you want to be in control?

My individualized consciousness is stronger than the pull of collective unconscious.

Day Six

Do you think the act of "doing" imprints the collective unconscious? For example, if you organize your desk, does this emphasize organization in the collective unconscious? Does this emphasize orderliness within the collective mind-pattern?

I refine my actions to positively imprint the collective unconscious.

Day Seven

I continue to develop my awareness of the collective unconscious upon myself and others. With awareness, comes responsibility for what I choose to put out for others to follow. Every day, spend a few seconds thinking about your choices—who will benefit (or not) and how.

I recognize that I am responsible for all that I add to the collective unconscious.

I am now aware of the collective unconscious.

Companionship

Day One

Have you allowed companions into your life who are not in your best interest? Who are they? Is it time to let them go? Have you learned your lessons from these people? If so, prepare these people on the Oversoul levels so they know that you are moving on.

I release all companions who are no longer appropriate.

Day Two

Do you use food, work, hobbies, or other things for your companions? Is this a way of satisfying your emotional needs without having to become too close to anyone? Are you ready to release these substitutes and move on?

I release all inappropriate substitutes for companions.

Day Three

To be a good companion to someone else, you must first be a good companion to yourself. Do you keep yourself so busy that you never have enough time to get to know yourself? Do you like being with yourself? What do you like about yourself?

I am my best companion.

Day Four

Do you take the time to visit with your Oversoul and God-Mind? Do you allow two-way conversations where you get answers to your comments, questions, and suggestions? Do you take the time to know how to interpret your inner communications?

My Oversoul and God-Mind are my companions.

Day Five

The outer world reflects your acceptance of yourself as a great companion. Where do you find these reflections in your daily life?

I find outer world reflections of my self-acceptance as a
great companion.

Day Six

Look for ways to open the doors to companionship in your life. Speak to others first, join a group, club, or discussion group. Become a volunteer in an organization that you believe in.

I open the doors for companionship to enter.

Day Seven

Who is your ideal companion? This might be a friend, neighbor, family member, spouse, or intellectual acquaintance. Only you know. Focus your thoughts, and concentrate on the following affirmation.

I give thanks for my ideal companion.

My Oversoul and God-Mind are my companions.

Compartmentalization

Day One
Society is becoming extremely compartmentalized in every aspect, from family and education to career and industry. Become aware of the compartmentalization of society, and thus yourself. Awareness allows you to change what you do not like.
I am aware of the compartmentalization of society, and thus myself.

Day Two
Careers are increasingly compartmentalized in an attempt to make the workplace more "efficient." This is one reason why so many people want to work for themselves. Being one's own boss is not necessarily so great and/or easy, but it is an attempt for people to bring wholeness into their lives once again. Can you see how the workplace is compartmentalized? How many examples can you think of?
I am aware of the compartmentalization of the
workplace, and thus myself.

Day Three
Families are compartmentalized. Family members are told, "If you are not happy, leave; leave your spouse, leave your children, leave your home." Tools in society to fix family units are not as easily accessible as tools to pull the family apart. Much is said and written about bringing the family together. Observe these platitudes to compare them with what is actually being done. This is how you are fooled—you hear one thing while something else really happens.
I am aware of the compartmentalization of the
family unit, and thus myself.

Day Four

Observe how the latest trend in the media is to flash scenes in front of your face. Before you have a chance to adequately focus, another scene is flashed. This keeps your thoughts defocused and scattered—another way of shattering the whole into compartmentalization.

I am aware of the attempts to compartmentalize by defocusing thoughts.

Day Five

Observe how the media plays on your emotions—the sexual nature of advertising, the fear that runs rampant in the news, anger fed–all attempts to take a variety of base emotions, feed them, and grow them into something that can be used against you. Open sexual chakras allow specific information to be programmed into the populace. People who are afraid willingly give up their freedoms. Angry people, especially a group of angry people, do things as a group that they most likely would not do as individuals.

I am aware of the attempts to compartmentalize via negative emotions.

Day Six

Food sources are becoming compartmentalized. Whole foods are less available and increasingly expensive. People replace whole foods with convenience in a scattered world. Take time to eat whole foods, symbolizing your acceptance of the whole you. Feed your body and mind the best whole nourishment that you possibly can.

I ingest whole foods to keep myself whole.

Day Seven

Continue to observe yourself to understand where you are scattered and defocused; how this is happening; who and what does this to you; and what part of yourself allows this. Take time to pull your thoughts, emotions, and lifestyle into the center of your being. Now that you are aware of the purposeful compartmentalization process, you can make conscious decisions to stop it.

I consciously make the decision to keep myself whole and complete.

I ingest whole foods to keep myself whole.

Compassion

Day One
With eyes closed, take a look at how far away from the body your aura extends. With your mind, will your aura in close to body. Mentally encase it in a bubble so that you have boundaries of where you start and where you stop. Fill the bubble with the color of compassion: pale pink. Feel pale pink permeate each and every cell of your physical, mental, emotional, and spiritual selves.
I fill myself with the pale pink color of compassion.

Day Two
Think about past difficult times when you had no choice but to be strong. Admire the fact that you survived; cry for the pain that these experiences caused.
I feel self-compassion for all past experiences.

Day Three
Think about the growth that came from your most difficult challenges. Think about how these difficult challenges forced you to grow.
I feel self-compassion for the lessons of difficult challenges.

Day Four
Make a list of your current challenges. Recognize that even though these challenges are important and worthwhile, they can sometimes make you feel alone and afraid. Feel compassion for your inner struggles.
I feel compassion for my inner struggles.

Day Five

Wear something pale pink, sleep under a pale pink blanket, and use a pale pink towel.

I bring self-compassion into my life.

Day Six

Accent your environment with pale pink. Bring in pale pink flowers, pillows, vases, photographs, and paintings.

My environment supports me with compassion.

Day Seven

Feel the softness of compassion filling your heart and soul. Know that compassion for Self means greater compassion for others.

I have deep compassion for myself and others.

I bring self-compassion into my life.

Conflict

Day One

Conflicts are a major source of division. The more conflict that exists within any given situation, the more the opposing forces like this. Where do areas of conflict exist within your life?

I identify areas of conflict in my life.

Day Two

Interpersonal conflicts take an amazing amount of human resources. You could use the same energy to propel yourself forward instead of stagnating in conflict. What are triggers for your negative reactions that keep you embroiled in a conflict cycle?

I identify personal triggers that maintain conflict cycles.

Day Three

Conflict is an opportunity for personal growth. Outer conflicts are a reflection of your inner state of being. Conflicts are tests that on some level you create for yourself to determine where you are in your growth cycle. Visualize yourself on the other side of the conflict. Once you move through this conflict, what do you think you will have learned?

I identify potential areas of growth from current conflicts.

Day Four

The more uncomfortable the conflict, the deeper you have to go inside to find the resolution. Conflict pushes you into areas of yourself that you did not even know existed. The more uncomfortable you are, the deeper you dig and the more resourceful you become. Sooner or later, you will find the answer and make your way through. Be proactive. Find the answer sooner rather than later.

I dig deep within my resources to resolve current conflicts.

Day Five

Physically relocating or moving someone out of your life does not resolve your conflict. This may give you a reprieve, but sooner or later, someone else will come into your life so that you can try again. Stay with the current lesson to release this and similar situations from your life on a permanent basis. Resolve the inner circumstances that create any life circumstance you do not wish to repeat.

I resolve inner conflicts to resolve outer conflicts.

Day Six

Conflict creates tension, stress, and eventually illness in the physical body. When you allow conflicts to settle into the physical body, you are the loser. Loosen up, relax, and prepare to take your test in a way that allows you to be in control of the conflict rather than the conflict in control of you.

I release all tension, stress, and illness associated with conflict.

Day Seven

Search out areas of your inner Self that are in conflict with one another. Create resolution in your inner world to ensure resolution in your outer world. Solutions may challenge you, but you are worth whatever it takes to complete your lessons. Do inner level work on the Oversoul level, prepare all involved, and put your world in order.

My inner and outer worlds are in order.

I identify areas of conflict in my life.

Confrontation

Day One
Many people avoid confrontation at all costs. Some people choose to hope that nothing happens. Some people take whatever blows life gives rather than confront issues that may make them feel uncomfortable. How do you feel about confrontation?

I identify my feelings about confrontation.

Day Two
How do you feel about confronting your own personal issues within? Do you take the time to deal with them, or do you avoid them? Are you willing to feel a little uncomfortable to resolve them?

I confront my own personal issues within.

Day Three
Do you confront your interpersonal issues? Or do you think that these issues will resolve themselves? Do you realize that everyone who plays a part in your interpersonal interactions is merely a reflection of you? If you do not confront these issues, the same type of person will continually manifest in your life. If you get rid of one person, another will pop up to take his/her place until you confront your own internal issues and bring them to a balanced conclusion.

I confront all interpersonal issues for a balanced conclusion.

Day Four
Do you confront your Oversoul with life circumstances that are unacceptable to you? Or do you passively accept whatever comes your way? Do you want to be a conscious co-creator of your life along with your Oversoul? If so, then speak up for yourself! Let your Oversoul know exactly how you feel about what is going on in your life!

I confront my Oversoul to become a conscious co-creator of my life.

Day Five

Do you confront the God-Mind within about how you feel about your very existence? Do you suppress your feelings? Do you feel that you have the right to let your Creator know exactly how you feel?

I confront the God-Mind within about how I feel.

Day Six

Do you confront issues only when you are forced to? Do you passively wait for situations to explode before you say anything to anyone? These can be internal explosions or external ones. Are you ready to release reactive confrontation?

I release the need for reactive confrontation.

Day Seven

Do you proactively confront issues? Do you do this with respect for others or are you belligerent in your approach? When you try to take care of yourself, do you think about how your words and actions affect others? Are you willing to learn to walk the fine line of balance that is necessary for successful confrontation?

I proactively confront all issues with respect for all.

I confront my own personal issues within.

Confusion/Doubt

Day One

With all that you know, all that you have read and studied, do you still find yourself confused about what to believe? Do you doubt what you thought was true or might be true? Are there life issues that still confuse you, causing you to wonder about correct decisions and how to make them? Gray is the color of confusion and doubt. Look in your wardrobe and surroundings to determine if you have gray colors, or colors with gray hues, that hold doubt and confusion in your life. If so, put the clothes and decorations away for the time being.

I release the need for doubt and confusion.

Day Two

Cleaning up the corners of your environment helps to remove the cluttered doubt from your mind-pattern. Every day this week, find a forgotten corner to sweep or vacuum out. These little pockets of physical confusion represent little pockets of mental confusion. A clear, clean environment removes the "gray areas" of your mind-pattern.

I easily identify and release hidden pockets of doubt and confusion.

Day Three

Unfinished projects need to be finished, disposed of, or given away. Keeping something that is unfinished means that you are confused. These symbols of doubt and confusion need to be removed from your life, one way or another.

I finish all projects.

Day Four

Today, make a definitive decision about something that you are procrastinating about. This could be a visit to the dentist, when to go shopping, taking a trip, or taking a specific class. Remove the confusion and doubt from your decision-making process.

I remove confusion and doubt from my decision-making process.

Day Five

Concentrate on moving energy vertically rather than horizontally. Prune trees and shrubs to grow up instead of out. Trim your hair so that it is "up" instead of straggly. Use jewelry, such as necklaces, earrings, and hair decorations to pull your energy "up." Replace horizontal stripes in décor and dress with vertical stripes. Anything that indicates upward flow in the physical world is a reflection of mental/energetic vertical flow. Living a "horizontal life" keeps you enmeshed in confusion and doubt, preventing clarity of Oversoul/God-Mind communication.

I create a vertical energy flow.

Day Six

Excess insulation on your physical body causes physical confusion and doubt, representing your mental/emotional confusion and doubt. Release the need for excess foods that support confusion and doubt. Make a decision today to eat in moderation (not eliminate your favorite foods!) and exercise to support the release of doubt and confusion.

I release all physical habits that add to doubt and confusion.

Day Seven

Give all doubt and confusion up to your Oversoul. Allow all the gray energy from your aura, and from every cell of your being on every level to flow up to your Oversoul. Let it go and watch it flow. Do this while you walk, talk, eat, shop, drive, and work. Use your mind as your tool to move confusion and doubt from your your physical space.

I release all doubt and confusion up to my Oversoul.

I release the need for doubt and confusion.

Connection

Day One

Breathe in from the top of your head to the base of your spine. Exhale from the base of your spine, out through the top of your head and up into your Oversoul. Visualize your Oversoul as a sun above your head that always stays clean.

I am connected to my Oversoul and God-Mind.

Day Two

Think of a situation that makes you nervous, or one that you avoid. Use your breath to confirm your inner connection. Look at the situation objectively, without angst or anxiety.

I am connected deep in the strength of my Oversoul and God-Mind.

Day Three

Think of a situation that upsets you, or creates internal panic. Use your breath to confirm your inner connection. Allow yourself to look at the situation objectively. Know that you access the appropriate actions at the proper time through your well-established Oversoul and God-Mind connections.

I am connected to the knowledge of my Oversoul and God-Mind.

Day Four

Using your spine as your guide, breathe in from the top of your head to the base of your spine. Exhale your breath up along your spine, up into your Oversoul and God-Mind. As you do so, feel your center, the point of reference from which your soul-personality operates.

I am connected and centered in my Oversoul and God-Mind.

Day Five

Practice your connection while performing your morning and/ or evening routines, driving your car, cleaning your house, or working in the garden.

I am consciously connected to my Oversoul and God-Mind at all times.

Day Six

Be aware of any situation that makes you feel like you are not connected to your Source. Whenever you feel this happen, breathe yourself back into your center before you respond. Use the situation to learn and grow. You are always connected, regardless of how you feel at the moment.

I am connected to my Oversoul and God-Mind every
second of every day.

Day Seven

As you perform your daily routines, think about all that you already know about people, places, and things. Think about how many times you have been "right" when you listened to your feelings. Think about how many times you have been "wrong" when you did not. Consciously acknowledging your inner knowing allows you to build on your existing deep inner connection.

I recognize and build upon my connection to Oversoul and God-Mind.

I am connected to my Oversoul and God-Mind.

Control

Day One

Do you feel sometimes like your life controls you, rather than you control your life? Do you feel like you constantly are running, trying to keep up emotionally, mentally, and physically? Do you feel drained and pulled in too many directions? If so, today is the day to stop and take control of your life!

I am in control of my life.

Day Two

Take control of your life by de-stressing. You cannot make thoughtful choices when you feel anxious and tense. Give yourself a timeout from the chaos. Make an appointment to see a massage therapist, chiropractor, acupuncturist, or reflexologist. Consider a day spa, or even a weekend away.

I take control of my life by learning to relax.

Day Three

Stop allowing the stressful events in your life to keep you wound up. Find even the smallest reason to welcome the upsets as opportunities for learning and growth. Know that you do not want to repeat these events again, so accept them, learn from them, and let them be your springboard into a new and better lifestyle. Take control of the stressful events in your life.

I am in control of all events in my life.

Day Four

Are your monthly bills overwhelming? Do you cringe when you get your credit card statements? Make a decision to take control of your finances. Sell something to pay off your obligations, take an extra job, transfer balances from one credit card to another for lower interest rates, balance your checkbook, and open a savings account, even if only for a small amount. Do something to install a new mind-pattern so that you can take control of your finances.

I am in control of my finances.

Day Five

Build up your physical health. Take a good daily multi-vitamin, decrease your intake of sugar and caffeine, strive for balanced eating over the course of a day or week, release the need for excess weight and insulation, and walk when you can, adding a little exercise.

I am in control of my body.

Day Six

Build up your mental health. Exercise your mind daily. Do hyperspace and Oversoul visualizations, surround yourself with supportive people, delve deeper into your hobbies and activities that increase enjoyment of life.

I am in control of my mental health.

Day Seven

Once you are in control of your life, and your life no longer controls you, then give your life to your Oversoul and God-Mind. Align yourself with your Source so that you can work together to bring you into your next level of awareness and growth.

I give control of my life to my Oversoul and God-Mind.

I am in control of my life.

Creating the Present

Day One
Whatever you think right now sets the stage for what happens tomorrow. Use your mind to bring your ideals to fruition. Live your life as if what you desire already exists—because somewhere, it does! Use allergies as an example. If you tell yourself that every spring your allergies act up, you set the stage for this spring, the following spring, and every spring from here on out. Your mind was powerful enough to create the allergies in the first place, so it has to be powerful enough to reverse the process.

I live my life as if what I desire already exists.

Day Two
How would you feel if you got that new job? Would you feel better about yourself? Have more self-esteem and self-respect? Visualize yourself there, surround your visualization in brown, and know that if this is the job for you, it is already yours.

I enjoy my job and the satisfaction it brings me.

Day Three
Ready to move? Pull your energy out of your current home. Visualize or feel your energy attaching to the new residence. Feel yourself there. Visualize violet cords holding you and any others who may be moving there. Ask that your current home be blessed, cleaned up, and be prepared for its rightful owners. On the Oversoul level, ask that the rightful owners come and claim their home.

I live in the home that I desire.

Day Four

Selling your car or other items? Physically clean them. As you do so, visualize all of your energy that was in that object going up to your Oversoul. Ask that these items be blessed, cleaned up, and prepared for their rightful owners. On the Oversoul level, ask that the rightful owners come to claim whatever it is that you no longer need.

I sell these items to their rightful owners for wonderful prices.

Day Five

What does it feel like to be in relationships that are healthy and promote self-worth? Visualize these relationships, surrounding them in brown to bring them into physical reality. Accept nothing less than what you deserve. Something is not always better than nothing. Rather than grab at the first relationship, wait for the correct one. Release the parts of yourself that are not able to enjoy healthy, healing relationships.

I am in healthy, healing relationships.

Day Six

What does it feel like to be free of debt? Visualize all debts paid in full and money in the bank. Mentally surround this with brown to bring it into the present.

All my debts are paid in full and I have money in the bank.

Day Seven

Visualize the life that you would like to live, with the people you would like to be with, and the financial structure you would like to have. Now, release it all up to your Oversoul. Ask your Oversoul to teach you how to bring this, its equivalent, or something better into fruition. Prepare yourself, your mind-pattern, your emotions, and your mind to accept this life.

I live the life that I deserve.

I live the life that I deserve.

Creativity

Day One

Creativity is centered in your right-brain. Creativity is propelled forward from your lower chakras, specifically your first (pale red) and second (pale orange). Within your creativity is your freedom of self-expression. When your lower chakras are held open via artificial means such as ELF and a bombardment of outside stimuli, your creativity becomes sidetracked. You feel stifled without a proper outlet for expression. Check your chakra bands. Release up to your Oversoul all the excess red and orange that exists within these chakra bands.

My chakra bands are in balance and enhance my creativity.

Day Two

Check yourself daily, or even several times a day, to ensure that the chakra band colors are correct. Flush yourself in violet to remove the residue of any ELF. Keep yourself centered so that your lower chakra bands cannot be over-stimulated. Limit your exposure to sexual stimuli that opens your creativity in an incorrect manner. When creativity stays bound in your lower chakras, it cannot move upward into the crown chakra to be manifested into physical reality.

My creativity correctly manifests into physical reality.

Day Three

Nutritionally support your creative chakra bands. Males need 50mg of zinc daily. Most females need 425mg of wild yam root on days they are not menstruating, one aloe vera capsule, and one black cohosh capsule. Add one blue cohosh capsule on days that you menstruate. Or, both males and females can take one teaspoon of royal jelly daily.

I nutritionally support my creative chakra bands.

Day Four

How are you creative in a negative way? Perhaps you are good at manipulation, game-playing, or destroying your body. Once you realize how creative you can be in a negative way, redirect that energy upward into positive creative pursuits.

I redirect negative creative energy into positive creative energy.

Day Five

How are you creative in a positive way? Are you creative in your work, finances, relationships, organization, fashion, design, art, reading, or children?

I identify my positive creative outlets.

Day Six

What are your dreams and goals for yourself? Whatever you can dream already exists somewhere in some reality. Use your creative energy to transform your dreams into reality. If you want to be an executive, buy an executive pen. If you want to be a chef, cook. If you want to be an artist, paint or draw. Open up the creative path.

I now creatively actualize my dreams.

Day Seven

Your creative ability already exists within. Open the flow to unleash the power of your potential creativity. Feel the creative flow in every cell of your being. Allow the flow to be so strong that you have no choice but to manifest your inner desires in this reality. Start in this moment. No matter how small or insignificant the step may seem, this opens your path in this reality.

My creativity flows strong, swiftly manifesting in positive ways.

I now creatively actualize my dreams.

Cycles

Day One

Everything has a cycle: a beginning, an ending and some move-ment in between. When a cycle follows its natural course, it creates an upward moving spiral. One cycle leads to the next, to the next, and so forth. Sometimes instead of moving through a cycle and onto the next, you get stuck. This creates a cycle that goes around and around in a circle that never ends. Take a look at your own life to determine if you have cycles that need to come to an end.

I release the need to hold onto completed cycles.

Day Two

Make a list of positive and negative cycles that you are tired of experiencing. These cycles literally "run you around in circles." Look in your closet to see if you have any clothes with horizontal stripes that go around and around. If so, could these be indicative of your current mind-pattern?

I identify all cycles that need conclusion.

Day Three

Release the energy of your completed cycles up to your Oversoul. As you pass this energy up, objectively observe each cycle that you consider complete. Identify the positive and negative learning gained from each cycle. When your feelings are neutral, or in balance, you objectively observe the cycle without your emotions coloring the information that you receive.

I release all completed cycles up to my Oversoul and God-Mind.

Day Four
Take a look around your physical environment to see if you hold onto old reminders of cycles now complete. Physically remove these items from your physical space, symbolizing mentally removing the old, completed cycles from your mental space.
I release all reminders of cycles now complete.

Day Five
Make a list of all unfinished projects waiting for completion. These unfinished projects represent cycles in your mind-pattern that are ready to be brought to conclusion. Finishing these projects in the outer world means conclusion of mind-patterns that have served their purpose. Today, choose one unfinished project and begin steps to complete it.
I bring all unfinished cycles to their natural conclusion.

Day Six
Make a list of new cycles that you wish to bring into your mental and physical environment. Anchor that cycle in with something physical—simply writing it down provides an anchor, or you can choose something like a picture, plant, or any item representing the new cycle that you wish to establish.
I anchor new cycles into my life.

Day Seven
Develop an awareness of the spirals of upward movement. Notice where you were: cycling around and around in a circle. Observe how new cycles build upon old ones. Create new cycles that move in an upward, spiraling motion.
I create cycles that move in an upward, spiraling motion.

I now creatively actualize my dreams.

Deficit

Day One

What kind of mind-patterns do you hold onto that keep you in a deficit situation? Start making a list so that you can release them.

I identify and release mind-patterns that keep me in a deficit.

Day Two

What kind of mental health issues do you insist upon holding? Do you set situations up so that you always feel like you are in a deficit? Do you recognize recurring patterns? Is it time to let them go and do something else?

I release mental health issues that keep me in a mental deficit.

Day Three

Do you use your programming as a way to excuse your behavior? Are you greater than your programming or is your programming greater than you? Who allowed the programming to occur in the first place? Do you respond to the general programming of society, thinking that "everybody else does it"? Do you want to be like "everybody else" or do you want to be like you?

I release programming issues that keep me in a deficit.

Day Four

Do you like being in a financial deficit? Are you really? Or are you responding to what society says is "financial deficit"? Does your mind-pattern allow for a financial deficit? Is it time to release this so that you can allow abundance in from all areas of your life?

I release financial issues that keep me in a deficit.

Day Five

Do you have physical issues that keep you in a deficit? Do you use supplements to maintain the physical system? Do you over-use supplements? Do you exercise and keep physically fit within reason? Do you have health issues that you perceive to be chronic and/or incurable? Do you know that the mind destroys the body and thus can rebuild the body?

I release physical issues that keep me in a deficit.

Day Six

What kind of issues do other people give you that put you in a deficit? Why do you choose to accept their words and actions? Do others give you issues or do you take these issues on willingly? What mind-patterns do you hold that allow others to put you in a deficit?

I release interpersonal interactions that place me in a deficit.

Day Seven

Do you have a stubborn tendency to hang onto issues when they are done and over? Is there a part of you that identifies with being a martyr and plays "poor me"? Does holding onto these types of mind-patterns create a deficit in your life? Is it time to release this aspect up to your Oversoul and move on?

I release martyr mind-patterns that hold me in a deficit.

I release financial issues that keep me in a deficit.

Depression

Day One

At some point in life, everyone goes through bouts of depression. Some people pass through these faster than others. Know that you are not alone in your experience, even if it seems that way. Whatever you experience, many have experienced before you, and many will experience after it is behind you. There are many simple things that you can do to move through these feelings. The first sounds easy, but when depressed, it may not be so easy for you: smile! Force yourself if you must. Use your fingers and pull up the sides of your mouth if necessary. Smiling releases specific endorphins in the brain that improves your attitude!

I feel the sunshine of my soul.

Day Two

Wear bright and uplifting colors. Avoid dark colors that might use you and pull you into depression. Even black writing pens can be depressing! Look around your home space. Clear up dark places. Think about painting areas that are dull or dirty.

I feel bright and uplifted.

Day Three

Sing songs that make you feel good. Even children's songs can be great upliftments. Make up your own tunes and words if you do not know any. Create deep tones to release your depression; create higher tones that promote upliftment.

My soul is in tune and harmony.

Day Four

Balance your T-Bar archetype, spin your chakras, go for a walk, get some sun, or even artificial light if natural light is unavailable.

My left-brain and right-brain are in balance.

Day Five

Work in your yard or garden, trim up any dead leaves on your indoor plants, throw out dead plants, bring new plants into your environment, and pick up a bouquet of flowers at your local super-market. Enjoy!

I enjoy and cultivate the garden of my soul.

Day Six

Be amongst other people. Do not sit home and procrastinate. Go to a mall, a grocery store. Find someone else that needs help more than you. Volunteer, even if it is only once.

I give freely of myself.

Day Seven

Get a haircut, color your hair, find new makeup, paint your fingernails, pierce an ear (or two!), put on some jewelry, call some friends, take someone to lunch, or ask someone in for lunch.

I lighten myself up in every way possible.

I feel the sunshine of my soul.

Direct Awareness

Day One
Feel your increased ability to know by knowing as your pineal gland area is balanced, harmonized, cleansed, and expanded. Feel the connection at the top of the head all the way up into your Oversoul and God-Mind. Understand that in your state of knowing by knowing, you gain your own information through direct awareness.
I learn through direct awareness.

Day Two
Develop confidence in your own abilities to understand and learn through direct awareness. Recognize how much you know without anyone other than your Oversoul and God-Mind confirming your inner truths.
I confidently access truthful information by direct awareness.

Day Three
As you learn to focus on what you already know, recognize that you can reach even deeper into your mind. This allows you to bring what you already know on a subconscious level into your conscious mind. You already see auras and everything that they contain. You see auras so fast that you do not know how to focus on what you see. Your subconscious mind sees auras and knows all. Bring this information forward.
I bring forward what I already know via direct awareness.

Day Four

Your subconscious mind connects to your superconscious mind. Your superconscious mind links to your Oversoul and God-Mind your Source and storehouse of all knowledge. When you decide to focus on your Source, you garner information through direct awareness. Why go to another person for their interpretation of your outer world when you can directly access your own Source?

I connect to my Source and storehouse of knowledge
with direct awareness.

Day Five

Visualize and feel your connection to your Oversoul and God-Mind. When you want an answer, mentally place your question at the pineal gland. Observe what comes into your mind. If you get a partial answer, do not think that you have something and something is better than nothing. Continue to focus on the question until you are satisfied with the answer. You can access your own answer through direct awareness.

I access my own answers through direct awareness.

Day Six

Think about a book that you have read. Place the book at the pineal gland. Ask your Oversoul to show you the true nature of the book. Know if the book is valid or not through your own ability to discern truth.

I learn discernment through direct awareness.

Day Seven

You can study any subject, person, or thing via direct awareness. Choose your questions wisely. Choose what you need to know over what you want to know. Through direct awareness, you always have access to any answer that you need.

I always have answers via direct awareness.

I learn through direct awareness.

Discomfort

Day One

Growth can be extremely uncomfortable, even when it is for the best. Letting go of whatever you have chosen for your teacher is like letting go of an old security blanket. Even if you do not like your current situation, you still know what it is and how to react to it. People choose all kinds of things for teachers, from health issues and pain to parents and other relationships. What teachers are you holding onto and why?

I acknowledge all teachers that bring me discomfort.

Day Two

What part of you requires discomfort for growth? How has this followed you all of your life? Are you ready to release this? Are you ready to step out and try something new and different?

I release my need for teachers that bring me discomfort.

Day Three

During growth, there is going to be discomfort. The old ways do not work well any more, the new ways are not yet comfortable. You know that you cannot go back, yet there is a part of you that does not want to move forward. You wind up in a push-me, pull-me type of situation until you make that final leap of faith. Are you willing to jump?

I am willing to be uncomfortable in the midst of my discomfort.

Day Four

Are you tired of repeating the same cycles over and over again? Are you tired enough of these cycles to let them go? Review your life, and think about how many times you have addressed the same situation over and over again. Are you ready to address new situations? Which is worse—to remain in the old ways, or to try new, unfamiliar ways?

I agree to experience the discomfort of unfamiliar territory.

Day Five

Stepping out into new growth means that old habit responses work less and less. You need to develop new responses to new situations. Others will be uncomfortable because they must develop new responses to your new actions. The chain of events affects everyone and everything in your circle. Are you willing to allow others to experience their own discomfort?

I let others experience discomfort when necessary.

Day Six

Movement and growth means change. Change means that new avenues of action must be explored and developed. Sometimes this is a quick process and sometimes it is a slow process. Whatever it is, you can learn to greet the discomfort as signs of growth and change.

I appreciate discomfort as signs of growth and change.

Day Seven

Not knowing exactly what to do or how others will react is an adventure. This is part of the exploration of the God-Mind. These challenges help you determine your own strengths and weaknesses, as well as define who and what you are, where you are going, and what you can someday be. Rather than label these feelings as "discomfort," begin viewing them as explorations of Self.

My discomfort evolves into self-discovery.

I acknowledge all teachers that bring me discomfort.

DNA Activation

Day One

Spin your chakras and balance your T-Bar archetype before doing any of the DNA activation exercises. If you feel trauma at any time during any of these exercises, surround yourself with brown, and immediately end the exercise. Focus on your pineal gland area. Place the DNA archetype at your pineal gland area. It looks like a ladder. Understand that utilizing this archetype activates certain DNA sequences that tell you who and what you are. Once these sequences are open, life-changing information is released and will affect you on all levels.

I comfortably open my DNA sequences.

Day Two

Spin your chakras and balance your T-Bar archetype. Now, place a medium green DNA archetype in your left-brain area. In your right-brain area, place a violet "Pi" sign. Using the Pi sign as a key, insert it into the DNA archetype. As the DNA archetype opens, visualize a pale yellow frequency line from the pineal gland into the open archetype. Take a few seconds to download the information. Next, place the Pi key back on the right-side of your brain. Notice if the DNA archetype stays open or closes.

I allow locked DNA sequences to open.

Day Three

Repeat yesterday's exercise. Repeat it as often as you wish. Remember that you have an infinite number of DNA sequences locked within. The more you repeat the exercise, the more information comes forward into your conscious mind.

I receive messages from my DNA sequences.

Day Four

Visualize a medium green spiral staircase, representative of your DNA. Move your consciousness down the staircase. When you come to a door, open it up and go in. This is something from your linear past that you need to explore and understand. If you feel trauma in any way, surround yourself in brown and come out of the experience.

I unlock experiences from my linear past.

Day Five

Visualize a royal blue spiral staircase, representative of your DNA. This time, move your consciousness up the staircase. When you come to a door, open it up and go in. This is something from your linear future that is important for you to understand. If you feel trauma in any way, surround yourself in brown and come out of the experience.

I unlock experiences from my linear future.

Day Six

Visualize a violet spiral staircase, representative of your DNA. Move your consciousness in any direction that you would like. When you come to a door, open it up and go in. This is something from your multidimensional Self that is important for you to understand. If you feel trauma in any way, surround yourself in brown and come out of the experience.

I unlock experiences from my multidimensional Self.

Day Seven

Visualize a royal blue circle with a dot at the pineal gland area. Place a medium green DNA archetype at the area. Ask you Oversoul to show you your true genetic history, from now to your original creation. You may or may not have any immediate answers depending upon what you are ready to know. As with all the other exercises, if you feel trauma in any way, surround yourself in brown and come out of the experience.

I explore my DNA sequences that contain my genetic history.

I comfortably open my DNA sequences.

Doubt

Day One

As you move along your journey, you most likely have little doubts along the way. Am I doing this correctly? Am I making any progress? Should I really be doing that? The doubts that can surface into a person's mind can be endless. These little doubts are really products of your various sub-personalities that are learning right along with you. While the core group is certain and determined, all the sub-personalities need to be addressed, not suppressed. When they speak, listen to them, discuss the situation with them, and then release it all up to your Oversoul.

I address my doubts.

Day Two

All doubts are important. They represent parts of your soul-personality that have not completed their learning. They are as much a representation of God-Mind as the forward moving sub-personalities. Breathe yourself into your center, anchor yourself in your Oversoul and God-Mind. Allow your doubts to speak. Their concerns may be valid—you may learn something that you ignored or avoided. As an objective observer, listen carefully rather than dismiss your doubts.

I objectively listen and learn from my doubts.

Day Three

Doubts can be fed by confusion. Clearing your physical environment results in clearing your mental and emotional space. As you work through doubt, avoid the color gray, which is a confusion color. Do some dusting—dust represents the little doubts of your life.

I move through my doubts with clarity.

Day Four

All the doubts that manifest in the outer world are simply reflections of your own inner fears. When you work through anything, someone or something will come try to dissuade you from moving forward. Learn to act correctly for the correct reason.

My doubts act as signposts and guides.

Day Five

Identify the difference between correct action and being led astray by doubt. Today, think about the things that you did not do because doubt stopped you, and you wish you had moved forward. Remember the feelings behind your lack of action. Remember the feelings behind the consequences of your decisions.

I use doubt wisely.

Day Six

How will I feel if I act upon my doubts? How will I feel if I do not? Now, project yourself into that "future" timeline. How do you feel if you act upon your doubts? How do you feel if you move through your doubts? Objectively explore all aspects of your doubts.

I objectively explore all aspects of my doubts.

Day Seven

Every thought that enters your mind does so for a reason. Study these thoughts, using them to teach, direct, and guide you. Never suppress them, because they are a part of you. Welcome your doubts as opportunities to learn balance for the overall soul-personality.

I allow my doubts to balance me.

I address my doubts.

Dreams

Day One
Dreams are messages from hidden parts of Self pushing way into your conscious mind. Remembering and understanding dreams are important aids to understanding who and what you are. Keep a notebook or journal by your bed, along with a small flashlight. The minute that you wake up, record your dream. If you wake up in the middle of the night, write your dream while it is still fresh in your mind. It is easy to forget even the most vivid dream as the day goes by.

I diligently record my dreams.

Day Two
Everyone dreams, whether you consciously remember them or not. Before you go to bed, utilize the following affirmation to help remember dreams. Write down everything that comes into your mind upon awakening, even if it is just bits and pieces, without making any sense. Immerse yourself in brown the minute you wake up to bring your dream memories into the present. The more you write down, the more you eventually remember.

I remember every dream detail upon awakening.

Day Three
Once you are accustomed to recording your dreams, it is important to understand their messages. Everything in your dream is a reflection of you, no matter how small. Even if you dream about people, places, or things that are familiar, these are representations of something meaningful. What do specific people, places, or things that you dream about mean?

I understand the symbolism of my dreams.

Day Four

Nightmares are messages that urgently need your attention. Rather than be upset by them, understand that these are especially important messages. These may be buried messages from your childhood, sub-personalities, or alters. Acknowledge these messages. Then, send them up to your Oversoul, ask for explanations, and record your thoughts.

I learn from all my dreams.

Day Five

If you have nighttime experiences when you are neither sleeping nor fully awake, flush your room with violet, put yourself in a violet tetrahedron inside of a violet octahedron. Breathe yourself into your center and know that nothing can enter into your consciousness unless you allow it.

I am protected during the night.

Day Six

As you study dream symbolism, take some time to study the symbolism that exists in your waking life. Pay attention to the details in the same way you pay attention to your dream details. In this way, you begin to understand that sleeping and waking are essentially the same.

I understand the symbolism of my waking life.

Day Seven

Go to your Oversoul for aid in remembering your dreams, as well as for explanations of the messages. Learn to read the symbols in the same way that you read words on a printed page. You already know everything. There is a part of you that knows the entire dream as well as its specific meaning. Ask your Oversoul to connect you with that part of Self so that all that you need to know is instantaneously revealed. Write in your dream journal every day, even if it is only one or two words. Eventually, your dreams clarify and you understand their messages.

I know and understand all my dream messages.

I learn from all my dreams.

Ease

Day One

When you are accustomed to learning and growing through struggle, you can feel odd when the struggle no longer exists. There is a part of you that questions if you can even grow without struggle. Because of this, it is easy to recreate the struggle even when it is no longer necessary. This is what you know. When you give up something, you must replace it with something or you pull the old ways back in. Are you ready for your life to flow with ease?

My life flows with ease.

Day Two

There are many paths to your journey's destination. You can take a smooth, straight, paved path, or you can take a narrow, twisty, rocky, dirt path. Each path has different experiences. Are you ready to take the smooth, straight, paved path?

I take the easiest path on my journey.

Day Three

Do you look at other people's lives thinking how much easier their lives could be if they would only do certain things? If so, this is a reflection of your own life. Whatever you see in others is only a reflection of you. Allow their complexities to teach you about your own life. In this way, you open up to easier paths in life.

I find my easiest path by observing other people.

Day Four

Are you experiencing any difficulty in your relationships—personal or professional? Is there an easier route? Is there a part of you that holds onto the difficulty? Are you ready to let that go so you can grow into something more?

My relationships flow with ease.

Day Five

Are you experiencing financial difficulties? Do you want an income increase? Do you feel stuck or stagnant, or perhaps feel like you are going backward? Are you in the process of defining your next step?

My finances flow with ease.

Day Six

Are you experiencing any health issues, either pronounced or subtle? Is your body healthy? Do you want to get even healthier? Do you have the correct healthcare professional to guide you through these issues? Are you responsible for the physical health of someone else?

All health issues resolve with ease.

Day Seven

With the proliferation of disinformation, do you feel confused and misled as you search for your answers? Sifting through information, do you wonder what to believe or not believe? Are you coming to the realization that the only person who has the correct answers for you is you? Do you wonder exactly how to pull these answers into your conscious mind?

Answers come to me with ease.

My life flows with ease.

ELF

Day One

ELF means "extra low frequency." These are frequencies that affect everyone every day. ELF is primarily transmitted through communication devices, such as telephones, radios, computers, and satellites. The degree to which you are affected is a direct result of many factors, from your location to your personal receptivity of these waves. ELF can disrupt your personal energy field, physical health, and mental capacities. It is important to be aware of its existence. Today, focus on all the electronic devices that surround you on a daily basis. Focus on the device that you see, and the communication transmissions through it that you do not see.

I am aware of extensive ELF in my environment.

Day Two

ELF transmissions usually show as bright or mustard yellow in your aura. If you have anything in your environment in these colors, they will attract ELF. Prescription medications and often some herbs also attract ELF into you. Review your environment to determine if you have anything that might attract and hold ELF. If so, is it possible to eliminate or modify these items?

I allow only pale yellow in my environment.

Day Three

The color violet eliminates and deflects ELF. With your mind, will your aura in close to you body. Place a violet bubble with a mirror on the outside around yourself to deflect ELF transmissions.

I deflect all ELF.

Day Four

Routinely flush your environment with violet to remove its residual effects. Use violet around the electronic devices in your home and office to neutralize ELF transmissions coming through them. Use violet on your travels, whether it be via car, bus, train, ship, or plane.

My environment is free of ELF.

Day Five

Sea salt baths, or swimming in salt water, negates the effects of ELF. Sea salt stabilizes your aura as well as draws toxins out of the body. Craving salt may indicate that your body needs to detoxify, or it may need the minerals that only high quality food-grade sea salt can provide. Sea salt also aids in mitigating radiation poisoning.

I release all residual ELF effects.

Day Six

To receive ELF, there must be a part of the mind-pattern that allows it to enter. Correct the holes in the mind-pattern that allow it to enter. The basic mind-pattern that allows ELF is victim-mentality.

I release the need to accept ELF transmissions.

Day Seven

You are the master of your ship. Everywhere you turn, others may try to push you overboard, but it is up to you to decide what to accept. Sometimes the decisions are not easy. You are the only one who can save you. No one else can. Make choices that are correct for you. ELF is designed to bring you down, but is is simply another test for you to walk through unscathed and unaffected.

I only accept that which enhances my Self.

I release all residual ELF effects.

Ending Old Cycles

Day One

To end cycles, learn absolutely everything that you could possibly ever want to know about them, both positive and negative. Make a list of all the things that you want to change. Noting both the positive and negative aspects of each cycle.

I end all old, unnecessary cycles, never to repeat them again.

Day Two

Make a point of eating everything that you want in the next few days. Satiate yourself to the point where you truly do not want to fill yourself like this again. Recognize that every piece of food you put into your body is a reflection of what you put into your mental house.

I end the cycle of ingesting unhealthy mental food.

Day Three

Think about all the parts of yourself and others that drive you crazy. Recognize that you criticize and judge others due to feelings of low-self worth. Stop the cycle.

I end the cycle of judging and criticizing Self and others.

Day Four

How many ways are you a victim? Do others treat you well? Does everybody else get what they want but you? Is someone else advancing at work, but not you? Do you wind up in the slowest moving lanes of traffic or shopping lines? How many ways are you a victim? Why do you attract this to yourself?

I end the victim cycle.

Day Four

Think about old habit responses that you use on a daily basis. Maybe you say "yes" when you want to say "no." Maybe you answer others' questions that you find too personal. Maybe you are too quick to anger without thinking first. What old habit responses are you ready to end?

I end all old habit responses that are no longer appropriate.

Day Five

Throw out old, useless objects that you keep in your home or office space. Perhaps you have inkless pens, old computer files, old clothes, dead plants, or old food in the refrigerator. Every useless object that you throw out represents useless cycles that you are ending.

I end all old, unnecessary mental cycles.

Day Six

Choose something to organize – a desk drawer, closet shelf, cupboard, coat closet, or glove compartment in your car. This represents organizing your mental house. Fill your body, mind, and soul with medium green for growth. When you end something, you must fill it with something, or you will feel empty and invite the old back in.

I fill my every cell with medium green for new growth.

I end the victim cycle.

Establishing New Cycles

Day One
Make a list of all the changes that you foresee for yourself. Prioritize your list by determining the most realistic goals. Devise a plan to actualize your goals. For example, rather than say that you will organize the house, think about organizing one room. If you want to organize your kitchen, think about organizing one area, or one cupboard. Instead of trying to accomplish giant leaps that in reality may be overwhelming or time-consuming, do a baby step, or one-half of a baby step that you can and will accomplish. Then do another half-step and so forth. Establish a new cycle of accomplishment.

I establish a new cycle of accomplishment.

Day Two
Listen to the world around you, recognizing that it is a reflection of your own mind-pattern. Rather than shut it out, listen and let it teach you. Establish a new cycle of letting the outer world teach you.

In my new cycle, the outer world teaches me.

Day Three
Surround yourself with people, places, and things that make you feel good about yourself. Remove yourself mentally and/or physically from anyone or anything that tries to make you feel less. Know that you pass these tests that you set up on the inner levels for yourself.

I establish a new cycle of high self-esteem and worthiness.

Day Four

Make a list of all the things that you do not like about yourself. Think of ways to bolster these weak areas to create an impenetrable mental fortress. Establish a new cycle of strengthening weak mind-patterns.

   I establish a new cycle of strengthening weak mind-patterns.

Day Five

Make a list of all the things you like about yourself. Think of ways to make those strong areas even stronger. Establish a new cycle of fortifying all strong mind-patterns.

   I establish a new cycle of fortifying all strong mind-patterns.

Day Six

Balance your T-Bar every morning and night. Spin your chakras as needed.   Surround your aura with a violet bubble with a mirror on the outside to deflect any negativity sent to you. Establish a new cycle that says, "I am impenetrable!" Know that you are protected on all levels.

   I establish a new cycle of protection.

Day Seven

Do something new today, no matter how small. Wear a new piece of clothing. Eat a food that you have never tried. Walk a different path. Be creative in a new way.

   I establish a new cycle for new solutions, ideas, and pathways.

In my new cycle, the outer world teaches me.

Evening Routine

Day One
With your hands extended above your head, stretch up high on your toes. Drop back down on your feet, keeping your hands in the air. Sway your hands back and forth; then, drop them to your sides. Slowly bend over and hang from the waist for a few seconds, not trying to touch the floor. Feel the gentle stretch of the spine. Slowly straighten up by stacking one vertebra on top of the next.
I am flexible, and open to the growth my night brings.

Day Two
When you get into bed, balance your T-Bar archetype located at your pineal gland. This brings the left and right-brain hemispheres into balance. Or, you can choose to use a royal blue circle with a royal blue dot in the middle to balance the brain hemispheres.
I balance my T-Bar to balance my brain.

Day Three
Flush your entire system with medium green to oxygenate, replenish, and rejuvenate as well as break up any energetic knots. Allow all that you no longer need to flow out the top of your head to your Oversoul. Repeat as needed.
I oxygenate, replenish, and rejuvenate my entire system.

Day Four
Create a protective violet bubble with a mirror on the outside around yourself others, and your home for nighttime protection. Or, you could use the ultimate protection technique, or a combination of both.
I sleep safely through the night.

Day Five

Place a brown merger archetype at the pineal gland. Use this archetype to integrate all parts of Self that may have been compartmentalized by you or others.

I merge all parts of Self.

Day Six

Release the energy of the day up to your Oversoul by quickly allowing your experiences to pass before your inner eye. Continue passing these experiences out through the top of your head and up into your Oversoul.

I release my day to my Oversoul.

Day Seven

Ask your Oversoul to prepare you for your night and your night to be prepared for you. Ask your Oversoul to help you remember your night learning the next morning, including your dreams.

I am prepared for my night.

I am flexible, and open to the growth my night brings.

Expansion

Day One

Rather than let the outer world close you off from your Source, now is the time to expand your horizons. Greet the challenges of your outer world. These are the challenges that create growth and strength on all levels.

I expand my horizons and embrace new growth.

Day Two

If you can survive and surpass in these times, most likely you can survive and surpass anything. This reality and its experiences are designed to bring you down. Be determined to create your own reality that propels you through the densest energies into the highest possible levels.

I expand my consciousness to reach the highest levels.

Day Three

Embrace the tough situations and people in your life from a proactive position to finally move beyond your own limiting mind-patterns. Proactively create easy expansion and growth into fabulous new mind-patterns without limitations.

I proactively create easy expansion and growth.

Day Four

If you can imagine something, it exists somewhere. Bring your desires to you by increasing and expanding your abilities on all levels. Know within yourself that you are unstoppable.

My abilities increase and expand on all levels.

Day Five

You are already connected to everything. You already know everything that you need to know. Increase your awareness of what you already are. Practice interpreting the energy behind spoken words and visuals. Expand your awareness of the inner knowing that already exists within.

I expand my awareness of my inner knowing.

Day Six

Refuse to buy into the mind-control of the collective unconscious that says jobs are scarce and you are laden with debt. You are one person, you need one job. There is an abundance of funds waiting for you to collect. Expand your financial abilities to pull to you exactly what you need, plus more than you can possibly envision. There is enough for everyone.

I expand my vision of career and finances.

Day Seven

Are you limiting your vision of what a relationship is as well as your ability to attain and maintain one? What does this say about you? Expand your definition of relationships. Give them all to your Oversoul and God-Mind, knowing that all your relationships now exist in ways that are fully enriching on all levels.

I expand my view of relationships.

I expand my consciousness to reach the highest levels.

Family

Day One

Everyone in your life is a reflection of you. Each person represents opportunities for growth. Families often gather during holidays, celebrations, and birthdays. Some people welcome these gatherings while others dread the thought of either being with family, or being alone. Do you consider the people who come to these gatherings positive or negative influences?

I objectively observe my family relationships.

Day Two

Which family members do you consider to be positive influences? Realize that these people are reflections of you. They take the time to show you who and what you are. On the inner levels, extend your gratitude to them, knowing that they add to the richness of your life.

I thank my family for providing positive self-reflections.

Day Three

Which family members do you consider to be negative influences? Realize that these people are also reflections of you. They take the time to show you who and what you are. On the inner levels, extend your gratitude to them, knowing that they add to the richness of your life.

I thank my family for providing negative self-reflections.

Day Four

As a microcosm of the macrocosm, you contain both positive and negative. All parts of Self are equally important. You can learn equally as well from the positive and negative people in your family. Sometimes, the negative family members teach you more than the positive ones! Everyone teaches you about you.

I learn from all my family members.

Day Five

Each family member represents an opportunity for growth. Accept the challenges that each person represents. Take a deep breath, and actively socialize with any person that you consider a negative. Give yourself a chance to objectively observe this person as a reflection of your own inner qualities. As you visit, ask your Oversoul to identify the qualities that each family member reflects back to you.

I welcome the growth opportunities from each family member.

Day Six

Do you have any emotional rifts with family members that need healing? These emotional rifts in the outer world represent emotional rifts in your inner world. Take the time on the Oversoul level to deal with your emotions. On the Oversoul level, speak to these people. Explore the possibilities of repairing these rifts so that you can allow your own inner lesions to heal.

I heal all rifts generated by family members.

Day Seven

Do you have any family members from whom you are geographically or emotionally separated? Would you like to bring these people back into your life? Explore the feasibility on the Oversoul level. Decide if this is the time. Decide if you are ready and if he/she is ready; then do what is necessary. If the person is no longer on this physical plane, you can communicate on the Oversoul level to bring your relationship to the correct place. .

All my family member relationships are in their correct place.

I objectively observe my family relationships.

Father

Day One

Most people have some kind of "father" issue. This is because your father provided you with one-half of your genetic material which allowed you to manifest in this reality. The genetics that you received from your father correspond with your mind-pattern at the time of conception. Because of this genetic connection, most people have a longing to know their biological father. How well do you know your biological father? What was active within him that attracted your mind-pattern at the moment of your conception?

I understand my father's mind-pattern at the
moment of my conception.

Day Two

If your biological father is no longer a part of your life, or if you have a stepfather or an adopted one, what are your mind-patterns that created these situations? Did you emotionally and logically understand why you chose these situations? Do you emotionally and logically understand them now? Do you have parts of Self that hold onto feelings that no longer serve a purpose?

I assess my primary father figure relationship.

Day Three

How is your current relationship with your father? Or, if he has passed away, how was it at the time of his passing? Does/did he have the ability to "push your buttons"? Do/did you accept him for what he is/was? Do you have a picture in your mind of what you want(ed) him to be and then when he is not/was not, you are/were disappointed and/or hurt?

I accurately assess my current relationship with my father.

Day Four

How has the imprinting left by your father figure affected your relationship with other males? Do/did you have unresolved issues with him? Do/did you question his motives and intentions? Do you constantly recreate your relationship with your father with other males? Do you treat other males as your father treated you?

I identify my father's imprinting and its affect on
my male relationships.

Day Five

Do/did you feel loved by your father? Is this okay or not? How does this affect love for Self? How do you extrapolate this onto others? If you do not think your father loves/loved you, do you think you deserve love from anyone, including Self? Do you feel that your father loved you the best that he could under his unique set of circumstances?

I understand the love of my father.

Day Six

Are you always seeking your father's approval in one form or another? Does this bring up any rejection issues? If so, how do you extrapolate this onto others? Do you constantly seek approval from others? Do you set up self-sabotage routines so you never receive the approval you are looking for? What do you repeatedly recreate around your father's imprinting that you no longer need?

I self-approve.

Day Seven

Working through your "father" issues and resolving them on all levels represents resolving and balancing your earliest mind-pattern imprinting. This allows all relationships to resolve and balance.

I resolve and balance my father issues.

I understand the love of my father.

Fear

Day One

Today, think about the words that you speak and hear, and the conditions that they create and enforce. Specifically, listen for the phrase, "I'm afraid...I can't do that, I don't have the time." How many times a day do you hear, "I'm afraid, I can't, I don't have"? What does this say about the mind-pattern of the person who speaks these words?

I observe the mind-patterns my words create.

Day Two

What are the negative aspects of fear? Do you have regrets about what you did not do because fear held you back?

I release the need for excess fear.

Day Three

Little fears are like roots attached to one giant fear tree. You might be surprised how much fear governs your life. What are you consciously afraid of? Are you afraid of not getting a good parking space, not having enough time, not finding the right piece of clothing? Are you afraid of heights, water, snakes, the New World Order?

I release the excess roots of fear up to my Oversoul.

Day four

The color of excess fear is a pus-colored yellow. Not a pretty sight! Pull your aura close to your body; put a violet bubble around it with a mirror on the outside. Allow the excess fear to flow and flow up to your Oversoul. Observe your aura as it becomes cleaner and lighter.

I release the color of excess fear up to my Oversoul.

Day Five

Excess fear creates holes in the mind-pattern that allow outside influence and manipulation. Make a list of your worst fears. Include your "If this happens, what would I do" kind of fears. Mentally go through the list, visualizing the worst possible scenarios and outcomes, continually releasing your thoughts and feelings up to your Oversoul. Mentally experiencing your fears can change your need to outpicture them into physical reality. Repeat this exercise until you do not elicit any reaction. At this point, you are neutral, and the excess fear is dissipated.

I release my worst fears up to my Oversoul.

Day Six

Fear in its proper place is important. Fear makes you stop to think before acting. You do not want to rid yourself of fear; you want to keep fear in balance. What are the positive aspects of fear? How has fear been your ally? When has fear stopped you from doing something that you were grateful that you did not do?

I recognize the positive aspects of fear.

Day Seven

Keep an eye on your mind-pattern of fear. This mind-pattern can only grow out of balance if you feed it. Little fears add up to big fears that can paralyze your ability to think and act. Release what you do not need up to your Oversoul as it occurs. Do not give fear the opportunity to grow out of proportion.

My mind-pattern of fear is in perfect balance.

I recognize the positive aspects of fear.

Filters

Day One

Regardless of what happens in life, you view every experience through your own internal filters. Before events reach your mind for interpretation, they pass through your wall of past experience, becoming increasingly distorted. You can clean your outer world filters to begin the process of cleaning your inner world filters. For example replace or clean your furnace filter, water filter, clothes dryer filter, or any other filter or filter-type object that you have in your home or office.

I recognize that I have internal filters.

Day Two

If you have a bad day, and someone speaks to you, you may interpret their words as "bad" when it is really your interpretation that is "bad." Your "bad" day colors everything that you hear and see.

I understand how my filters affect my interaction with others.

Day Three

Whatever your past experiences, you use them to interpret your world. If you had a difficult relationship with a parent, you may react to anyone with similar characteristics as if he/she is your parent. The person may be a perfectly innocent bystander, but because you need to release your past, you react as if your parent had spoken. Examine your relationships, from casual to close, to determine how your personal filters interpret your reactions.

I determine how my personal filters interpret my reactions.

Day Four

If someone speaks harshly, your filter may interpret their tone to mean that they do not like you. Perhaps that person has had a bad day and nothing personal is directed at you. Move your consciousness up to your Oversoul. Allow your Oversoul to be your filter.

My Oversoul filters the events of my world.

Day Five

How did your personal filters develop? Do you have issues with one gender or the other? Were these views influenced by a primary caregiver? Did you have a "bad" experience at some point that you relive over and over—say a "bad" dentist that brought you trauma? Now, whenever you sit in a dentist chair, your filters force you to relive that trauma.

I identify my personal filters and their points of origin.

Day Six

Release your unnecessary subjective filters up to your Oversoul. As you do so, observe how much clearer and cleaner the space around you becomes.

I release my unnecessary filters.

Day Seven

Recognize the effectiveness of your Oversoul as an information filter. Observe how much easier it is to stand in your center regardless of outer circumstances.

I always use my Oversoul as my filter.

My Oversoul filters the events of my world.

Finances

Day One
Money is symbolic of energy. Not having enough money to meet your needs is symbolic of self-denial. Think about how many times during the day you state, "I don't have…" This is a statement of your inner being.

I release the need for lack.

Day Two
Some people think that money is not "spiritual." Everything that exists comes from God-Mind, including money. Nothing in this world is more or less spiritual than anything else. Everything originates from the same Source. Money is a medium of exchange that greatly simplifies the exchange of personal energies. When you think of money in the terms that it is "non-spiritual," you are denying a part of God-Mind, and you drive it away from yourself.

I accept money as a part of God-Mind..

Day Three
Maybe someone told you that you would never amount to anything, or perhaps implied it. All kinds of things are said to people in their developing years that belittle inner self-worth. Take a look inside. Find those statements, pass them up to your Oversoul, and release them permanently. Forgive those people, for they were truly ignorant of the long-term effects of their words and actions.

I am worthy of money.

Day Four

Feel the reality of having ample funds for whatever you desire: a new wardrobe, new car, paying off your bills, or money in the bank. Visualize the experience. If it is a new wardrobe, mentally buy it, bring it home, put it in your closet, and wear it. Feel the excitement of sitting in a new car. Feel the relief of your bills all paid. Look at the large balance in your bank account. Manifest your desires.

I experience God-Mind's abundant supply of energy.

Day Five

How many times do you think or say, "I never have enough…time, energy, milk, gas." These words plant a very specific mind-pattern that needs to be removed. Watch your words and thoughts.

I always have enough.

Day Six

Do you cringe when the mail comes? Do you procrastinate viewing your bills? Do you set them aside to look at them "later?" Rather than avoid your bills, acknowledge them. Visualize each bill paid in full, with money left over.

My bills are now paid and I have money left over.

Day Seven

Not having enough money may be the impetus to change directions in life. Something is squeezing your life situation to the point where it is not working. Maybe it is time to refocus your energies in another direction. This might be what you need to open the floodgates of abundance.

The floodgates of abundance are open.

I always have enough.

Flushing With Colors

Day One

Brown is a great color to ground and stabilize yourself when you become nervous or anxious. Flush your entire system with brown to bring calm into the present moment.

I flush myself with brown to bring calm into the present moment.

Day Two

Flush yourself with medium green to oxygenate the physical body as well as balance your emotions.

I flush myself with medium green to oxygenate and balance.

Day Three

Flush yourself with the pale pink of compassion for unconditional love. Allow pale pink to permeate every cell of your being.

I flush myself with pale pink for unconditional love.

Day Four

Flush your brain, eyes, nose, and ears with royal blue. This color balances the brain and heals vision and hearing as well as your sinuses. Royal blue strengthens this part of the body.

I flush my brain, eyes, nose, and ears with
royal blue for strengthening.

Day Five

Flush your entire system with violet to cleanse and protect the physical body, as well as deflect ELF.

I flush myself with violet to cleanse and protect.

Day Six

Flush yourself with silver to aid in your conscious Oversoul connection. Continue to observe how much lighter, clearer, and cleaner you feel on all levels.

I flush myself with silver to connect every cell to my Oversoul.

Day Seven

Flush yourself with gold to consciously connect to God-Mind and the wisdom It contains. Recognize that you are never separate from God-Mind. Develop your conscious connection so that you know by knowing all that you ever need.

I flush myself with gold to establish my conscious connection with God-Mind.

I flush myself with pale pink for unconditional love.

Focus

Day One
"These are trying times." How many times have you heard this? Yet, when you think about it, was there ever a time in history when "trying times" did not exist? Review your own life. You may find that you have had more "trying times" than not. How did you get through these times? Most likely, only with the strength of your own internal focus.

My internal focus gets me through trying times.

Day Two
When times are most trying, you do not stop to evaluate how you get from Point A to Point B. You simply go. Trying times often put you in survival mode. Sometimes, it is only after the fact that you stop to realize what you came through. When you focus and direct your concentration, it is amazing what you can do. Become the objective observer. Think about your trying times. Give yourself credit that you made it through.

My focus moves me effortlessly through life.

Day Three
Can you maintain your focus regardless of outer world activity? Do you want to go to a quiet mountaintop to connect Self, Oversoul, and God-Mind? Do people, places, and things agitate you because you see them as roadblocks to inner "enlightenment"? Realize that what you want to go away are opportunities to teach you to focus no matter what else bothers you.

I use outer distractions to develop a strong inner focus.

Day Four

Utilize every opportunity to strengthen your focus. Where can you go, what can you do, and still maintain your focus? What are you doing in your life right now that requires focus? Cooking, driving, sports, hobbies, and reading all require focus.

I use every opportunity to strengthen my focus.

Day Five

What one goal would you like to accomplish? Have you tried to attain it before? How was the strength of your focus? Did you allow anyone or anything to distract you? To be successful at attaining your goals, visualize your goal at the pineal gland. Focus on the end result, allowing your goals to come to you.

My focus brings my goals to me.

Day Six

There is an intense bombardment of ELF every day and all through the night. Some people experience personal ELF attacks. The ELF is designed to distract and de-focus you. Think about the times when you allowed this to happen. Develop your sensitivities so that you know when you are bombarded. Allow nothing to pull you off course.

The strength of my focus keeps me on course.

Day Seven

Think of the strength of your focus as an ice-cutter ship, cutting through the outside distractions with strength and ease, steadfast and powerful, in total alignment with the focus of your Oversoul and God-Mind. With such determination and power, you can get through anything.

The strength of my focus is steadfast and powerful.

My focus brings my goals to me.

Forgiveness

Day One

When others hurt you, logically you may understand what happened and why. On the emotional level, you may still feel like yelling or screaming at that person. Let those emotions loose... on the Oversoul level. Allow yourself to feel whatever you feel, passing those thoughts, feelings, and actions up to your Oversoul. When you no longer feel the need to emotionally vent, you are ready to proceed.

I forgive as I vent all emotions to my Oversoul.

Day Two

Holding onto feelings toward people who have hurt you continues to draw those people, or people with similar mind-patterns, to you. Visualize the cords and attachments that hold these feelings to you. Visualize these attachments falling away so that you are no longer connected to this mind-pattern in any way.

I release attachments so I can forgive.

Day Three

On the Oversoul level, tell anyone who has hurt you that you forgive him/her for all past actions. Check to ensure that there are no remaining cords or attachments between you.

I forgive everyone who intentionally and
unintentionally harmed me.

Day Four

Realize that anyone who harmed you was merely a reflection of your mind-pattern at that time. These people were teaching you about yourself. On some level, everyone involved agreed to the experience. Now, they are still teaching you about forgiveness.

I thank everyone who teaches me about forgiveness.

Day Five

On the Oversoul level, ask that the people who are teaching you about forgiveness be sent the help and direction that they need. Know that your part with them is over. Know that you will not attract the same type of people or the same painful lessons ever again. Know that it is possible to forgive anyone who brings you harmful, painful lessons.

I forgive everyone who brought me harmful, painful lessons.

Day Six

These experiences can only come came into your life with your permission. On some level, you are responsible for these experiences. If this makes you angry, take a minute to yell and scream at yourself for attracting these types of experiences. Pass these emotions up to your Oversoul. Forgive yourself for attracting harmful, painful experiences.

I forgive myself.

Day Seven

All people hurt each other from time to time; sometimes intentionally, most often unintentionally. When this happens, deal with the situation at the moment rather than allow your emotions to fester. Always vent your emotions, then move on, forgiving everyone involved.

I immediately forgive myself and others as needed.

I forgive myself.

Freedom

Day One
What does freedom mean to you? Do you freely move about your home? Is there anyone or anything within, or outside of, the home that prevents you from experiencing the freedom that you desire? How are these persons or things reflections of your own inner mind-patterns?

I create a mind-pattern of freedom.

Day Two
Do you have freedom of self-expression? Do you chastise yourself for your thoughts and limit your willingness to express them? Does someone else influence your ability to think and develop your own conclusions? Does someone else influence what you verbally express or do not express?

I allow myself mental and verbal freedoms of self-expression.

Day Three
Do you feel the influence of society upon your internal thinking process? Do you feel the thoughts of the group-mind? Do you feel the ELF that is directed at the collective? Do you feel like you need to go off by yourself to escape the influence of others?

I have freedom from societal influence.

Day Four
Do you move freely about in society without paranoia of bodily harm and/or attack? Do you understand that you are always in a place that reflects the safety within your own mind-pattern? Do you understand that you attract the outer experiences that are generated by your own internal feelings of self-freedom?

I have freedom to move safely within society.

Day Five

Do you allow others their personal freedoms? Do you try to infringe your beliefs, structures, or ways of doing things on others, either silently or vocally? The more freedom you give to others, the more freedom you give to yourself. They are one and the same.

I give others their personal freedom to obtain my own.

Day Six

Are you able to find a balance of personal freedom within society's freedom? Can you live freely within a society that only thinks that it is free? Can you allow society its journey without infringing your idea of freedom upon it?

I balance my personal freedom with societal freedom.

Day Seven

Continue to monitor your own internal thoughts and outward expressions. Utilize what you already know. Wherever you find your freedoms restricted, go inside to find the mind-pattern that generates the situation. Release the mind-pattern up to your Oversoul and God-Mind, moving on into full expression of your personal freedom.

I live and express all phases of my life in freedom.

I create a mind-pattern of freedom.

Fruition

Day One

Make a list of uncompleted tasks that you are avoiding. Take a step toward completing one of these tasks. Realize that you cannot bring tasks from the old level into the new level that you are in the process of creating. Bring past tasks to fruition so you can move on.

I bring past tasks to fruition.

Day Two

Make a list of goals in your new level of development. Who are you now? What do you expect to happen now that you are in a different space? What do you deserve? Why? What new goals do you plan to bring to fruition?

I bring my new goals to fruition.

Day Three

Make a list of your top three expectations for yourself and your life. Choose one expectation. Take a step toward bringing this to fruition. You may not make a "perfect" step. The result may not be exactly what you want, but at least it is one step. The best way to bring your expectations to fruition is one step at a time.

I bring my expectations to fruition one step at a time.

Day four

Banish all doubt. Whenever thoughts of doubt creep up, or you meet someone who encourages doubt, recognize these feelings as self-tests. When it is time for your efforts to come to fruition, this will happen without doubt of any kind. Be confident in your ability to bring your goals to fruition.

I confidently bring my goals to fruition.

Day Five

Realize that you are far enough into your next level that you may be tempted to go back into the old level. Old mind-patterns are more familiar than the current ones. Stay firmly on your path. Focus on what is before you, realizing that you have already learned from your past. Claim what you have worked for, acknowledging that you deserve to enjoy the fruits of your labors.

My new level of development now comes to fruition.

Day Six

Feel your inner strength. You may be unaccustomed to this new level of strength, but this is exactly where you belong. Do something different to symbolize your acceptance of a new way of living – eat at a different restaurant, shop at a different store, purchase a different type of clothing – anything that symbolically puts the outer life on a new level and path.

My outer life symbols bring my inner changes to fruition.

Day Seven

It is time to harvest the fruits of your labors; all of the hard work that you have done these past few years. These have not been easy times for anyone. You have been pushed to your limits and beyond. Stop, put your life in order, and bring to fruition all the seeds that you have planted. Gather some of the seasonal harvest, whether this be fruits or vegetables. As you eat these foods, recognize that they symbolize the fruition of your own personally planted internal seeds.

All my goals and desires now come to fruition.

I bring my new goals to fruition.

Genetics

Day One

Think about your birth family. Why do you think that you chose this particular family in which to be born? Think about what their genetics bring forth in you. Consider such things as physical features/characteristics, talents, and hobbies. What do you have in common with your family lineage?

I identify my family lineage expressions.

Day Two

Investigate your family lineage. Do you have a lineage of musicians, athletes, cooks, spiritual seekers, professionals, blue collar workers, emotional stability, or mental strength? How does your environment, and your family's environment, support this? Do such things as funding, location, "being in the right place at the right time," friends, and educational opportunities support these mind-patterns?

I know the environment that my family genetics create.

Day Three

At the moment of conception, what were the genetics that pulled you into this family? What genetics did you look for to enhance your mind-pattern at that time?

I know my family genetics at the moment of my conception.

Day Four

How does your lineage provide the opportunity for you to remain stuck in your mind-pattern? How does your lineage provide the opportunity for you to move through and "overcome" the imbalances in your mind-pattern? Can you identify these same basic traits and characteristics within your lineage; i.e., siblings, parents, grandparents, cousins, aunts, uncles? How specific can you get, such as grandmother, mother, daughter all getting pregnant before marriage, and so forth?

I understand the mind-patterns generated by my family line.

Day Five

What latent genetics do you have within that you would like to open and activate? How far back can you trace your genetics using only your mind? Close your eyes and focus at your pineal gland. Use the DNA archetype in dark green. See the rungs open. Move your consciousness into you own genetic codes.

I unlock my genetic codes to understand my mind-pattern.

Day Six

Know that your mind-pattern is stronger than your genetics. You can say that you can or cannot do something because of your genetics. You may be predisposed to a specific mental, emotional, or physical condition, but this is only because your mind-pattern pulled you into this genetic lineage. You can "break out" of that particular genetic programming.

My mind-pattern is stronger than my genetics.

Day Seven

You can use the strengths within your genetic gene pool to enhance and boost any of your natural, inherent abilities. Ask your Oversoul to show you any part of your genetic code that you may have overlooked that is important for your advancement within this reality.

My Oversoul directs and guides my genetic exploration.

I identify my family lineage expressions.

Geographic Frequencies

Day One
Every geographic location has a specific feeling, or frequency, to it. Focus your consciousness on the continents. Feel the differences between each one as you move your consciousness around the globe. Feel what North America feels like, then South America. Feel Europe, Asia, Africa. Feel Australia and Antarctica.
I identify global frequencies.

Day Two
Feel the oceans versus the land. Feel lakes versus rivers and streams. Move your consciousness around the global waters, just observing the differences.
I identify the frequencies of global waters.

Day Three
Feel the frequencies of mountains and volcanoes; the frequencies of canyons and earthquake fault lines. Feel the frequencies of deserts versus frequencies of foliage. Move your consciousness from place to place, feeling the differences.
I identify geographic frequencies.

Day Four
Feel on top of the land versus under the land. Feel the frequencies around large cities and under them. Feel the frequencies around small towns and under them. Feel the frequencies of national parks, natural formations, and caves. Move your consciousness around the Earth, feeling the surface and what is under it.
I fine-tune my abilities to identify specific geographic frequencies.

Day Five

Feel the frequency of the area in which you live. Feel the frequency of the town or city. Feel the frequency of the street and your home. Do the frequencies match yours? If not, how are they different? Is this a positive geographic location for you? Does this location pull you up into your potential, hold you where you are, or pull you down into something less than you desire for yourself?

I identify the frequency of my current location.

Day Six

If you are thinking about relocating, feel the frequency of the geographic location of your choice. Feel your own frequency to see if they match. What kind of experiences does this particular frequency bring?

I identify the frequency of my best geographic location.

Day Seven

Feel the frequency of every geographic location you go, whether it is in your home, yard, building, workplace, or street. Refine your sensitivities to all that is around you. Bring into your conscious mind all that you already know about these geographic locations. Do not judge or criticize, simply be aware of all geographic frequencies wherever you are.

I am always aware of my surrounding geographic frequencies.

I identify the frequency of my current location.

Giving

Day One

Think about all the people you remember with gifts and cards during the holiday season. How do you feel about giving? Do you look forward to the season, dread it, or feel neutral about it?

I am honest with my feelings about giving.

Day Two

Think about all the people you feel obligated to remember, but would rather not. Remember that these people reflect you. Acknowledging them keeps their reflection in your life.

I consciously choose to whom I give.

Day Three

Think about all the people you would like to remember, but cannot for whatever reasons. These people are also reflections of you. Not acknowledging these people keeps their reflections out of your life.

I give to those people who are positive self-reflections.

Day Four

Prioritize your card and gift-giving lists. Release those that no longer need to be on the list. Add those who you would like on the list. Acknowledge and set your boundaries by desire rather than through limitation.

I choose the recipients of my giving wisely.

Day Five

Think about why you give cards and gifts. Is it for pleasure, business reasons, guilt, because you think you have to, or for other reasons? Remember that whatever you give out comes back to you.

I give joyously.

Day Six

Think about the financial boundaries that you set for your giving. Do you stay within those boundaries? Or do you go beyond your own boundaries and wish you had not?

I respect my financial boundaries for giving.

Day Seven

Do you give yourself enough time to accomplish your goals? Do you feel rushed and panicky? Or do you enjoy feeling rushed?

I give myself enough time, energy, and resources to accomplish my needs.

I am honest with my feelings about giving.

Goals

Day One

Do you think about your long-term goals. When you are a child, you think about the future, and what you will be doing. But, once you are out of school and caught up in your career and life, sometimes you are grateful to survive the daily rigors. Do you still have long-term goals? Are they the same now as they were a few years ago?

I review my long-term goals.

Day Two

Do you have your goals in writing? Writing your goals down is a way to anchor them into physical reality. Today, write your goals on paper. What would you like to do a year from now? Two years? Five years? Ten years? Continue to follow the goal-setting as many years as you can envision.

I anchor my goals into physical reality.

Day Three

Do you set any short-term goals in your daily life, such as plans for the day, week, month, or year? If so, do you carry your goals through to completion? Use a daily planner book to write goals to anchor them into this reality. Accomplishing your goals in the short-term establishes a mind-pattern of goal accomplishment, including long-term ones.

I establish a mind-pattern of goal accomplishment.

Day Four
Use your goals as guideposts rather than tools for self-punishment.
Are there goals that you do not think you reached? Do you worry
about this, or use this as a "failure" so that you can feed low self-
worth issues? Perhaps what you attained was something different,
but not "worse." Take time to evaluate past goals to determine any
leftover feelings that may need to be released to your Oversoul.

I release leftover feelings of "goal failure" to my Oversoul.

Day Five
Are your goals realistic? Is "realistic" even important? What do
others tell you about your goals? Do you allow others to determine
your goals for you? Do others reflect your own personal doubts
and inner conflicts about your goals? Have you stopped reaching
for your goals because you accept the limitations placed upon you
by others?

I am the only one who determines my goals.

Day Six
Realize that your goals are your plans for your life. Your Oversoul
may be able to see something better for you of which you are not
consciously aware. Once you determine your goals, give them up
to your Oversoul for review and revision.

I give thanks for my goal, its equivalent, or something better.

Day Seven
Bring the goal clearly into focus so that it has no choice but to
come to you. Realize that everything is a reflection of your own
mind-pattern. When the strength of your mind-pattern is strong
enough, there is nothing that will stop that goal from reaching
you.

The strength of my mind-pattern pulls my goals directly to me.

I am the only one who determines my goals.

Graduation Classes

Day One
Many people are experiencing a great deal of travail in their lives right now. Good people with good intentions who accidentally let their guards down, or people with soft underbellies that other people have found and seem to enjoy poking. As rough as these lessons are, these are all self-invited for the purpose of growth. These are your graduation classes, and you must pass them to move onto your next level.

I accept the graduation classes that I chose.

Day Two
If you think about quitting, what are your alternatives? Do you think life gets any better if you do not complete your class? Would you have consciously signed up for these lessons? Can you review and identify at what point you selected this class?

I accept my responsibility for my graduation classes.

Day Three
What are your goals? What will you personally gain when you complete this course? Will you remember these lessons "forever"? When you get through this class and look at it from the other side, what will you know upon completion that you did not know in the beginning?

I explore all knowledge within my graduation classes.

Day Four

Do you sometimes think that "it cannot get any worse"? Release that thought up to your Oversoul immediately. Whatever is in your life, be grateful that it is not any worse, or any harder. Know that somewhere, some place, someone has it worse and harder than you do. Remember the old saying, "There but for the grace of God go I."

I am grateful for my graduation classes.

Day Five

You do not have any greater burdens than you can bear. Only a strong, intelligent person can self-design such difficult classes. You were strong enough to be willing to sign up for the courses, so you are strong enough to get through them.

I easily complete my graduation classes.

Day Six

You are not the first to have taken these courses, and you will not be the last. When you complete these graduation classes, you will have the opportunity to be finished forever with the mind-pattern that created these classes in the first place. You will have greater understanding and compassion for those who take these courses after you. You will be a better person for what you went through.

I pass my graduation classes to complete specifc mind-patterns.

Day Seven

At the conclusion of these classes, you will have the opportunity to walk another road within the God-Mind matrix; explore new and different knowledge; and reach places that heretofore were unimaginable to your conscious mind. Be grateful for the process that takes you to new heights and knowledge.

I give thanks for my graduation classes.

I accept the graduation classes that I chose.

Hopelessness & Despair

Day One

Do you have feelings of hopelessness and despair? Often, this is a result of ELF bombardment. Release the need to fall into this trap. You are stronger than ELF.

I release the need for feelings of hopelessness and despair.

Day Two

As you release the need for hopelessness and despair, you must replace it with something else. Otherwise, you will feel empty and pull these feelings back to you. Breathe out what you do not need; breathe in what you do need.

I replace feelings of hopelessness and despair with
centeredness and calmness.

Day Three

When you have overwhelming feelings of hopelessness and despair, it is easier to see only the negative in all things. Make a concentrated effort to focus on the positive. Even a "small" positive is the foundation for a new mind-pattern. How many "small" positives can you name? How many "large" positives? Can you list 100 of each?

I focus on the positive as I release hopelessness and despair.

Day Four

Do you see your cup of life "half full" or "half empty"? Spend the day perpetuating the mind-pattern of a cup "half full." Then, visualize your cup brimming over with all the wonderful things that you can imagine. Whatever you can visualize exists somewhere. Use the strength of your mind-pattern to create this as your reality.

My cup of life brims over with positive life experiences.

Day Five

Make a list of what you have, rather than what you "do not have." In God-Mind, all things exist. If you can visualize it, you can have it. With the accentuated ELF bombardment upon the masses, it is "easiest" to focus on what you do not have.

I focus and build upon all the positives that I have.

Day Six

When you feel torn apart inside, you need to get back into a place of self-integration. Place the brown merger symbol within each chakra band to reintegrate all parts of Self.

I integrate all parts of Self.

Day Seven

Anchor into the Angelic frequency portion of your Oversoul. Surpass the ELF bombardment of the Earth. You have been in the ELF long enough; you have total understanding of it. Stop playing in ELF; move beyond ELF. Use the silver infinity sign to pull you through hopelessness and despair and into a higher frequency.

I move through hopelessness and despair into a higher frequency.

I integrate all parts of Self.

Identifying Frequencies

Day One

Everything has a specific feel, or frequency to it. Today, simply observe that there is a difference between animate and inanimate objects, i.e., observe that a person and an animal have a different feeling, or frequency, than a desk and a rock.

I identify frequency differences between animate
and inanimate objects.

Day Two

Observe the differences in commercial frequencies. For example, schools have a different feel than hospitals. Schools and hospitals have different feels than banks. Do this with a variety of organizations and businesses, from funeral homes to churches. Understand that although there is a wide variety of commerce all around, each type has a specific feel, or frequency to it.

I identify the difference in commercial frequencies.

Day Three

Observe the differences between the types of people who work in various businesses and organizations. For example, a person working in a school has a different feel, or frequency, than one who works in a hospital. A person who works in a bank has a different feel, or frequency from a person who works in a shopping mall.

I identify the frequencies within fields of employment.

Day Four

People in the same fields of employment have similar frequencies. For example, medical professionals all have a similar "feel," or frequency. Finance people all have a similar "feel," or frequency. Choose one field of employment and feel the common frequency of the people within it.

I identify the common frequency of same-field people.

Day Five

When you go into any business, observe that there are clearly three primary frequencies present. The first is that of the employees. The second is that of the employer. The third is that of the customer. Feel, or identify, the differences between these three frequencies.

I identify three primary frequencies within all businesses.

Day Six

Observe the advertisements in newspapers and magazines. Observe that each advertisement has a specific feel, or frequency, to it. Some advertisements feel comfortable, safe, and inviting; others feel harsh, cold, and stagnant. When you view these advertisements, you react to something more than the printed word. Feel the frequency behind the advertisement. What type of business is it? What are the employees like? What is the physical environment of the business like?

I identify the frequency behind all printed words.

Day Seven

Observe the frequencies of your surroundings, including the buildings and/or homes that you pass. What kind of person works in that building, or lives in that home? What is the frequency of that specific person? Is he/she happy, sad, intense, struggling? Does he/she have low self-esteem or high self-esteem?

I identify the frequencies of buildings, homes,
and the people therein.

I identify the frequency behind all printed words.

Identity

Day One

Who are you? Do you identify with your mind-patterns more than your soul-personality? What mind-patterns bring you which issues? Do you create your identity around these issues? How would you feel if the issues suddenly vanished?

I release the need to identify with my issues.

Day Two

If weight is your identity, think about the consequences of losing it. Would you lose your "grounding?" Would you need new clothing? What kind of clothing would you buy? Do you have the nerve to wear what you envision? Would you be open to a new relationship? Would you have to give up your fantasy world and come back down to Earth? What other issues would weight loss include that perhaps on some level you wish to avoid?

I recognize the consequences of changing my current identity.

Day Three

If anger is your identity, what would be the consequences of bringing this emotion into balance? Would you have to examine hidden fears? Would you have to show your vulnerability? How many relationships would have to be recreated?

I recreate relationships to establish a new identity.

Day Four

If low self-worth is your identity, what are the consequences of having strong self-esteem? Would you expect more of yourself? Would others? Would you be thrust into an uncomfortable lime-light? What exactly would you give up by establishing a mind-pattern of strong self-esteem?

I create a new identify of strong self-esteem.

Day Five

What are the consequences of a victim-mentality identity? Do you always look for a reason to be upset or unhappy? Is there a part of you that enjoys being hurt? Could you function without this mind-pattern? Could you function in a smooth, happy life? What part of you feeds off victim-mentality?

I release victim mentality as my identity.

Day Six

What are the consequences of losing lack as your identity? Do you deserve to have positive abundance in every area of your life? Is your mind-pattern strong enough to pull in everything that you can ever possibly need? Would you still keep the same friends, or would they drop you? Would you have to find new places to shop and new topics of conversation? How would an abundance identity change your life?

I allow positive abundance to be a part of new identity.

Day Seven

What are the consequences of losing poor health as your identity? Would you get less attention? Would you be able to justify time and expense taking care of your physical body and emotional well-being? Do you deserve fabulous health? Would you still be the center of attention? Would a part of you lose control over others? Exactly how much would you lose by no longer identifying with poor health? What would you replace it with? Would you be successful?

I allow fabulous health to be part of my new identity.

I release the need to identify with my issues.

Information

Day One

This is an information age. No matter where you go, your senses can easily feel overloaded and overwhelmed. You may worry that you will miss vital, important information through all the external noise. To increase your capacity to receive vital information, place the Pineal Gland Archetype (royal blue circle with royal blue dot in the middle) between the eyebrows. Keep your brain in royal blue.

My balanced brain is receptive to vital information.

Day Two

Pale yellow is the color code used to absorb information. Mentally surround yourself in pale yellow. Allow pale yellow to permeate every level of your being to easily absorb information.

I surround myself in pale yellow to easily absorb information.

Day Three

Contrary to popular opinion, you can absorb information through osmosis! This can be positive or negative information. Surround yourself in violet so that only positive information comes into your mind.

I surround myself with violet as an information filter.

Day Four

Add a pale yellow frequency line from your pineal gland to a book, program, person, or place. This provides a direct connection to your information source.

I connect a pale yellow frequency line to my information source.

Day Five

Ask your Oversoul to direct you to information that is especially important and meaningful. Be mindful of how you spend your time. Keep informed, but make choices that are to your benefit.

I know how to find information that is meaningful to me.

Day Six

Let your Oversoul direct your knowledge of conventional and unconventional information. No matter what you are investigating or exploring, wait until you are told to go somewhere, read something, or take a class before you act. Learn to allocate your precious resource of time when information-gathering.

My Oversoul directs all my information-gathering.

Day Seven

What if you can see aura colors but do not know what it means? What if you have fantastic mathematical formulas but do not know what to do with them? Give everything that you know to your Oversoul so that your Oversoul can explain the information to you.

My Oversoul explains all information to me.

My balanced brain is receptive to vital information.

Inner Resources

Day One

Think about all the inner resources that you have called upon to get you to this point in life. Recognize that no matter where you are mentally, physically, emotionally, and spiritually, you have developed a cache of inner resources that you rely upon.

I give thanks for all current inner resources.

Day Two

When it is time to move into new levels of being, it is important to clear out the old resources that took you to your current level. Think about the old resources that you do not really need anymore. Release these up to your Oversoul and God-Mind.

I release all old inner resources that I no longer need.

Day Three

Ask your Oversoul to open your mind to a new level of inner resources—all inner resources that you need to move forward into new areas of being.

I open my mind to new inner resources.

Day Four

At first, you may think that there is nothing new available to you. But, your challenging circumstances will push you into new inner resources on a reactive basis. Or, you can take a proactive stance by pushing yourself inward to pull out what will better serve you now. Think about this; be prepared to make your choices.

I move continually deeper inside to access new inner resources.

Day Five

Once your new inner resources flow to the surface, think about old challenges that need resolution. Allow new avenues of action into your conscious mind based upon the new inner resources now available.

I resolve old challenges with my new inner resources.

Day Six

Recognize that your old foundation is now replaced with a new foundation upon which to actively grow.

My new inner resources create a new foundation.

Day Seven

With a new foundation in place, your new inner resources create an entire new level of being—make this a positive learning and growing experience. Let go of anything that holds you back. Now is the time to release procrastination and move forward.

My new inner resources propel me into new levels of being.

I give thanks for all current inner resources.

Insomnia

Day One
With the stresses and demands of everyday living, insomnia is a growing problem. The physical body must be well rested to deal with daily stresses, but the cycle of insomnia is self-perpetuating—not enough rest means a tired body that in turn means a less than optimal functioning mind. The mind-pattern behind insomnia is one of not allowing oneself to rest and relax.
I allow myself to rest and relax.

Day Two
Insomnia has a way of taking over your life. Before you go to bed, you know you will not sleep. The thought of not sleeping makes you tense before you lay down. While you may easily fall asleep on the couch the thought of going to bed creates tension. Your past thoughts have created tense energy around your bed. Every time you lay in bed, you feel this tense energy. Release this tense energy up to your Oversoul, replacing it with an energy that relaxes you.
I deserve to rest and relax.

Day Three
Change the placement of the bed in your room. If possible, change the sheets, blankets, and quilts. This resets the energy pattern. Stay up until you are sleepy, even if it is three or four in the morning. You may have to stay up all night and go through the next day. Only go to bed when you are about to fall asleep. This establishes a new energetic pattern in your bedroom that says, "This bed is for sleeping."
I deserve to sleep deeply, soundly, and restfully.

Day Four

Before going to bed, sit in a comfortable place to review your day. Start with the moment you got up in the morning until the moment that ends your day. Pass all your thoughts and feelings up to your Oversoul. Give these thoughts and feelings color, shape, weight, and consistency. Releasing them to your Oversoul removes the daily tension from your aura. Replace these daily tensions with a color that relaxes you.

I release the tensions of the day.

Day Five

When you get up in the morning, pass all your thoughts and feelings about the night up to your Oversoul. These thoughts and feelings have color, shape, weight, and consistency that you keep in your aura. Rather than carry any night tension with you, give it to your Oversoul. Replace it with a color that relaxes you.

I release the tensions of the night.

Day Six

Perhaps nightmares or night time experiences keep you from sleeping. When you sit to do your release work, look to see what is specific and unique to your refusal to allow yourself to rest. Allow that to come up and pass before your inner eye. Use the mental tools that you already have to resolve the situation.

I have positive night experiences.

Day Seven

Drink a cup of relaxing tea before starting your nightly release work. Do some gentle stretching exercises. Read a boring book to calm your mind. If you are really ready to let go of the cycle of insomnia, you cannot keep doing the same thing and expect different results. Developing a new night time routine changes your sleep patterns.

I sleep deeply, soundly, and restfully.

I allow myself to rest and relax.

Integrity

Day One

There are many ways that you maintain your integrity. The outer world has rules that you must follow or face the consequences. These keep you in alignment with the ways of society, whether you like the rules or not. There are societal organizations with established rules of integrity, such as the rules of church and family. Finally, you establish your own rules of integrity. What rules are important to you? What do you do when no one is looking, or when you think that you can "get away" with something?

I am responsible for maintaining my own integrity.

Day Two

How do you feel when you do not act with integrity? Do you feel satisfied that you "got away" with something? Who benefits and who loses? Where did this mind-pattern begin? Why is it important to you? Is there a part of you that feels like a victim? Does breaking the rules give you the feeling of control?

I release all blocks that prevent me from acting with integrity.

Day Three

Are you carrying mental and/or emotional weight from any areas of your life where you have not acted in integrity? If so, how can you correct this imbalance? Are you doing something now that you can correct? Decide within yourself how to correct any imbalances.

I correct all current integrity imbalances.

Day Four

If there are any past actions not carried out with integrity, what can you do to correct this? For example, if you took something that belonged to another, what can you do to rectify the situation? Can you discuss this on the Oversoul level with all involved parties? Can you give something of equal value to someone else?

I correct all past integrity imbalances.

Day Five

If you do not like the existing rules, use your own mind-pattern to help instigate change. If this is not possible, then move out of your current circumstances into a place where the rules are compatible with your own expectations.

Outer world integrity expectations match my
integrity expectations.

Day Six

Taking advantage of anyone for any reason opens the door for others to do the same. If you take something from someone that does not belong to you, whether physical, mental, or emotional, something will be taken from you to maintain the balance.

I align my integrity with my Oversoul and God-Mind.

Day Seven

Make a conscious decision to move forward with integrity. Be the master of your own mind. You know the rules, whatever they are. They exist for a reason. Always act in conscious awareness. Act with integrity because this is the correct thing to do. Allow the outer to reflect the inner, and the inner to reflect the outer.

I move forward with integrity.

I am responsible for maintaining my own integrity.

Interference

Day One

Do you have people interfering in your life? If so, then this is a reflection of yourself and your interference in the life of others.
I release the need for interference from others.

Day Two

Think about people who you have tried to help in the past, but who have rejected your help. Was this interfering in their lives?
I release the need to interfere in the lives of others.

Day Three

Did you have people ask you for help, only to have your advice turned down or even used against you at a later date? Learn to listen on the Oversoul level so that you know when people really want your advice and when they only want to complain without a true desire for help.
My Oversoul directs me when to help others.

Day Four

Most people spend a lot of time thinking out loud. They really do not want a response from anyone—they simply sift through their own ideas. Learn to let others talk, even when you have to bite your tongue to keep from offering advice. Silently, ask your Oversoul to deliver your advice on the Oversoul level in a way that the other person can hear.
I freely advise others via the Oversoul level.

Day Five

Listen to the feedback from your Oversoul. Your Oversoul teaches you when to verbally speak and when to only speak on the inner levels. If you are unsure and choose to verbalize your advice, observe the reactions of the other person. Observe body language, gestures, and words to determine how well your advice is received.

I easily discern whether to speak on the inner or outer levels.

Day Six

Sometimes the lessons that people set up for themselves are extremely difficult from a subjective point of view. There may be many times when you would like to take away someone's pain, heartache, and fears, but this may be exactly what that person needs to grow. Do not take away another's lesson, or you are the only one who learns.

My Oversoul explains to me all that I need to know.

Day Seven

No one can interfere in your life unless on some level you invite and allow the interference. Rather than be upset with these people, correct your own mind-pattern. No one can interfere in your life without your permission. Whatever you give out returns to you. Examine your own mind-pattern to determine where you are interfering. Correcting your own mind-pattern is the only way to prevent others from interfering in your own life.

I correct my mind-pattern to prevent interference by others.

I release the need for interference from others.

Internal Control

Day One

Most people are so bombarded from the world that they do not even know where their own thoughts originate. With your mind, create a violet bubble around yourself to establish boundaries as well as filter out electromagnetic transmissions.

My own boundaries establish internal control.

Day Two

Think about your most influential people—are they family, friends, peers, or co-workers? Do you live your life the way you want, or the way that others dictate? While it is important to listen to others, it is another thing to allow the opinions of others to override your own inner knowing. Who has the most influence in your life—you, or others?

I establish my own internal controls.

Day Three

How strongly do societal beliefs influence you? Do you think that you will become old and decrepit? Do you think that you should participate in self-deprecating behavior? Do you want to rush out to purchase the newest products advertised? How does society influence you, both positively and negatively? When do you allow society to exercise control over you?

I make decisions using internal control as my reference point.

Day Four

Do you "go along with the crowd" when you prefer not? Do you wish that you could freely state what is really on your mind? Do you determine correct behavior based upon the judgments of others? Do you go "against the crowd" just because you want to be different? Is this any better than "going along with the crowd"? Are you still allowing others control over you?

I evaluate all options via internal control.

Day Five

Do you read public opinion polls and surveys? Do these sway or influence your opinions? If the reports say that X% of people are depressed, or not sleeping, or using antidepressants, do you pick up these thoughts? Do you try to find a way to determine how you fit into the picture? Who authors these reports? What are their goals and purposes? Are they in alignment with yours? Are the external controls stronger than your internal controls?

My internal controls are strong, solid, and supportive.

Day Six

Attempts at external control are everywhere. List twenty attempts of your environment to control you, from media to family to ELF transmissions that interfere with the normal function of your brain waves and aura. As you develop your awareness, you increase your ability to maintain internal control.

I have 100% internal control.

Day Seven

Every day you are inundated with people trying to force external controls. How many times do you capitulate to their efforts, either consciously, or unconsciously? When you are pulled outward, you lose your own personal strength as well as reasoning and knowing ability. Build and maintain a mind-pattern that only allows internal control.

I am 100% internally controlled by Self, Oversoul, and God-Mind.

I have 100% internal control.

Invisibility

Day One

To be a part of anything, you must have an archetype, color, or tone in your aura that matches the situation. No one and no thing can enter into your frequency in any way unless there is a part of you that matches. That is why one house in a neighborhood can be compromised while all the others remain untouched. With appropriate colors, tones, and archetypes, you are invisible to any undesirable person, place, thing, or circumstance.

Appropriate colors, tones, and archetypes make me invisible.

Day Two

Have you ever looked for an address while driving, but could not find it? Do you drive by the same stores day after day, but do not know their names? This is because your archetypes, colors, and tones do not match the address you are searching for or any of the stores that you pass every day. Recognize that some places are invisible to you.

I recognize that some places are invisible to me.

Day Three

Depending upon archetypes, colors, and tones, some objects can be invisible to you. You can be in an entire library and never notice specific books. You can trip over toys in your own home. There are repetitive advertisements in newspapers that you never see. The list goes on and on. Stop to really look at your surroundings. How much of it do you really see?

I recognize that some objects are invisible to me.

Day Four

You can make yourself invisible by consciously clearing your aura of archetypes, colors, and tones. With your mind, will all contents of your aura to move into your center. Then pass everything up out the top of your head and up to your Oversoul to hold for you. Practice doing this to see what happens—but be sure you do this at the appropriate times!

> *I become invisible by removing archetypes, colors,*
> *and tones from my aura.*

Day Five

You can make your home and possessions invisible by asking that their respective archetypes, colors, and tones be passed up to your Oversoul to hold. Be careful what you choose and when—if others on the road cannot see your vehicle, for example, there could be a problem!

> *My possessions become invisible at the appropriate time.*

Day Six

You can mentally cloak yourself in black to hide the archetypes, colors, and tones. You can also do this with your possessions. Try this to see what happens.

> *I cloak myself in black to become invisible.*

Day Seven

If you do not wish to attract specific experiences, then do not carry the archetypes, colors, and tones to bring them in. Do your inner level work to clean out all that you no longer need. Essentially, this allows you to remain hidden and invisible to experiences in which you do not wish to participate.

> *I am invisible at the appropriate times.*

I am invisible at the appropriate times.

Know By Knowing

Day One
Everyone already knows everything; it is simply a matter of where you focus your attention. For example, right now, you know more information than you could possibly ever state. You know your name, age, address, and phone number. You know where you are sitting and what room you are in. When you take the time to consciously label all that you already know right now, it is pretty amazing.

I know by knowing.

Day Two
When you walk into your home, you know more details than you can ever possibly state. You know such things as where your furniture came from, what took place on which piece of furniture and stories connected with your special decorations. You automatically know this, and more, when you walk into your home.

I know by knowing a plethora of information.

Day Three
Pick up any object. Focus on what you already know about it. For example, a cotton towel – trace the towel back to its origins, step by step. Trace the towel's origins back to the farmer planting the cotton seed, to the store where the farmer purchased the seed, or even how the cotton seed came to the store. You can learn more about that towel by focusing and following its energetic thread. See how much you already know? You are not being "psychic" you are simply in a state of knowing.

I easily access information when I practice knowing by knowing.

Day Four

Think about a person other than yourself that you know well. Ask permission via the involved Oversouls to focus on that person. With permission, realize what you already know about that person, such as general behavior, personal habits, likes and dislikes, emotional and mental state, and health. Remember, this is what you know, not what someone told you. If this person tells you that he/she is in a great relationship and you see otherwise, this is your information. Use your know by knowing to go beyond words.

My know by knowing exceeds words.

Day Five

Look at a stranger on the street. Ask permission via the involved Oversouls to focus on that person. With permission, recognize what you already know about him/her. You have never met this person, yet you already know a myriad of information. Pay attention to clothing, body language, color, and the feeling of the energy that is around this person. What do you already know without ever uttering a word?

I know by knowing all things about everyone.

Day Six

Look at the outside of a house or apartment building. Ask permission via the involved Oversouls to take a look at the building of your choice for information about it and its occupants. How much do you already know?

I know by knowing all things about everything.

Day Seven

Never use your abilities to pry, or you will close down or be closed down; this is Universal Law. Recognize how much you already know every day. Recognize that you already function in a state of knowing by knowing – simply choose where you want to focus your attention.

I know by knowing with discretion and permission.

My know by knowing exceeds words.

Levity

Day One

With all the events in the outer world, sometimes levity gets lost in the process. Even when you are by yourself, spend some time smiling. Smiling releases endorphins in the brain that promote your sense of inner well-being.

I smile to promote inner well-being.

Day Two

Think of a joke or amusing story that makes you laugh. Share it with a friend or acquaintance. Laughter releases endorphins from the brain that promote your mental and physical health.

I enjoy light-hearted laughter with those around me.

Day Three

Wear some light-colored clothing to raise your spirits. Dark colors are good for grounding and depth, but they can also pull you down if you let them.

I wear light, uplifting colors.

Day Four

Look at your environment to see if you are surrounded by dark or light colors. Determine where to add light colors to add "lightness" to your life. This could be as simple as a vase of flowers or a pillow.

I fill my environment with uplifting colors.

Day Four

Find a fun place to spend some time. Choose a comedy club, amusement/water park, cruise, or any place where you can have some fun. Set a date and go!

I go to places that uplift my spirits.

Day Six

What kind of people surround you on a daily basis? Do these people pull you up into your potential, hold you where you are, or pull you down? Is it time to make decisions about who you want in your life or to discuss how you expect to be treated?

I choose people in my life who uplift my spirits.

Day Seven

Have you thought about getting a pet, or do you already have one? While pets are a lot of responsibility and should only be taken on with much thought, pets can be a tremendous boost to your inner sense of well-being. If a pet is not a possibility, spend some time simply watching the antics of others' pets or observing wild creatures. Perhaps think of volunteer work among animals.

I allow pets/animals to uplift my spirits.

I smile to promote inner well-being.

Like-Minded People

Day One

When you feel lonely, remember that being alone pushes you into yourself and thus into your Oversoul and God-Mind. Turning inward is a positive step toward self-reliance.

I rely on my inner support system of Self,
Oversoul, and God-Mind.

Day Two

As you gain Self support, this support is reflected back to you by the outer world. Your world may be filled with "closet" like-minded people. Tell your Oversoul that you are ready for like-minded people to make themselves known to you.

I allow like-minded people to enter my life.

Day Three

Look around at your current support system, or lack thereof. Who do you hold onto that does not support you? Why do you need these types of people in your life? If you let these people go, will this make room for others who will support you? Closing one door opens another.

I open the door for like-minded people to enter my life.

Day Four

Re-assess the people in your life. They may have more interests similar to yours than you realize. Ask your Oversoul to show you beyond their words. Feel the deeper energy that emanates from the inner Self. Is this inner Self receptive to information "outside the box"?

My Oversoul shows me the inner Self of like-minded others.

Day Five

Explore the part of you that is used to being alone. What are the positive aspects of being alone? What are the negative aspects? Do you really want a support system of like-minded people with the realities that it brings? More people mean more complications. Do you want to deal with the complications? Do you deserve a support system of like-minded people? Are you ready to accept the positive and negative attributes of like-minded people?

I am open to a support system of like-minded people.

Day Six

Once you agree to allow like-minded people into your life, then you must open the doors to allow them in. Observe how you block these doors from opening. Use the strength of your mind-pattern to automatically draw like-minded people into your life.

The strength of my mind-pattern draws like-minded people to me.

Day Seven

Allow the strength of your mind-pattern to reflect back to you via the people that you know. Perhaps others are waiting for you to move so that they can change and grow. Perhaps the strength of your mind-pattern will be reflected back to you via new inner strength in the people you already know. Recognize that you may now have created the pathway to deeper levels of communication with others already in your life.

I communicate with people I know on deeper, like-minded levels.

I allow like-minded people to enter my life.

Living Example

Day One

Everyone is a living example of something. As the song on the Expansions *Peace In The World* CD says, "What do you want to teach? Who do you want to reach?" Think about all the people that you influence every day simply by being. Everyone sees everything about everyone, regardless if they acknowledge it consciously. What kind of a living example are you?

I observe and evaluate myself as a living example.

Day Two

What does your physical appearance say about you? Are you neat, clean, and well-groomed? Are your clothes disheveled? Are you somewhere in between? What does your symbolism teach others?

My physical appearance is a positive living example.

Day Three

What does your method of transportation say about you? Do you keep your vehicle clean and neat, inside and out? How is this reflective of your own mind-pattern? How does it influence others? If you use public transportation, how are you a living example to those around you? What do you teach simply by being present in the space of others?

My method of transportation is a living example.

Day Four

What does the way that you carry yourself say about you? Do you walk with your head held high or low? Are your shoulders back with a straight spine, or pushed forward with a sagging spine? Do you look people directly in the eye or avoid their gaze? Do you have a spring in your step or do you shuffle and drag your feet? What kind of example is your deportment?

My deportment creates an uplifting living example.

Day Five

What does your environment teach others? Do you think your home can influence the homes around you, as well as those within it? What about the outside of your living space—what does that teach? What about your work environment? What do you teach others through your environment?

My environment is a positive living example.

Day Six

What do you teach through the tone in your voice? Do you teach patience and kindness? Do you teach honesty and forthrightness? Do you teach compassion and understanding? Objectively listen to yourself to determine if you like the living example that exists through your voice.

My voice is a living example of wisdom,
tolerance, and compassion.

Day Seven

Whether you know the people around you or not, whether you see others once in your life or several times a day, you are a living example to anyone who comes in your space. Every second of every day, you determine what your living example will be. Think about what you teach others so that you can decide in conscious awareness what kind of living example you want to be.

I consciously define my living example.

I observe and evaluate myself as a living example.

Loneliness

Day One

Do you feel lonely without anyone to share your innermost thoughts? Do you feel isolated and unaccepted even when you are in a group of people? Do you feel that you will never belong? Do you make statements of isolation through your body language, the way that you arrange your environment, or even the way that you dress? If you feel lonely, how do you project this statement into the outer world to promote and maintain these feelings?

I am aware of how I maintain loneliness.

Day Two

Do you feel emotionally isolated from friends, family, spouse, children, and people in general? Do you feel that you emotionally give, but do not receive? Is there a part of you that does not feel it can emotionally receive? Why? Where did this mind-pattern begin? How can you correct it?

I emotionally receive from others.

Day Three

Do you feel intellectually isolated from people with whom to share your ideas, interests, goals, plans, and passions? Do you have low self-worth issues that question your ability to intellectually interact with others? Is it easier to remain intellectually isolated and alone?

I intellectually receive from others.

Day Four

Does your physical locale promote isolation? Why do you choose a location that keeps you separate from others? Is there safety in loneliness? Is that easier than to risk rejection by others?

I live close to like-minded people.

Day Five

As with all things, there are positive reasons for allowing a time of loneliness in your life. For example, loneliness pushes you away from the "collective" or group-mind, into individualized consciousness. You recognize that you are separate from others.

I give thanks for lessons learned from loneliness.

Day Six

Loneliness forces you to become your own companion; to appreciate your intricacies, nuances, and eccentricities. Loneliness forces you to know yourself—both the positive and negative sides; the richness of your own fabric.

I appreciate the richness of my own soul-personality.

Day Seven

Loneliness pushes you into yourself, where you find inner communication with your Oversoul and God-Mind. Out of need and desire, you develop your inner focus, giving you strength and fortitude that might not otherwise be attained.

My connection with Self, Oversoul and God-Mind
is deep and ongoing.

I emotionally receive from others.

Long-Term vs. Short-Term

Day One

Too many people want "quick fixes" for situations that require time and patience. Most people do not think beyond getting through the day, week, month, or possibly even year. What kind of "quick fixes" do you focus on? What do you want changed "yesterday"? What sacrifices do you make because of your willingness to accept short-term solutions?

I identify the sacrifices of short-term solutions.

Day Two

Do you give up your long-term health for short-term fixes? Do you take antidepressants or recreational drugs to feel good today without consideration for their long-term effects? Do you choose not to exercise because you are too tired today without thinking about the long-term negative effects? Do you give up long-term benefits for short-term solutions?

I choose long-term benefits over short-term solutions.

Day Three

Are you willing to give up the short-term pleasure of "junk" food so that your body feels better long-term? Are you willing to take the time to prepare more "whole foods" and give up the short-term benefits of chemical-laden prepared foods? Are you willing to take a good daily vitamin supplement so that your body maintains its long-term health?

My wise choices bring long-term quality of life.

Day Four

Do you accept "any" type of relationship as a short-term solution to your loneliness? Do you continue to repeat these same types of relationships rather than be alone for any length of time? Are you willing to be alone for a while, work on yourself to create, manifest, and draw to you a long-term relationship that is mutually beneficial, satisfying, and long-lasting?

I prepare for long-term fulfilling relationships.

Day Five

Do you take "anything" jobs for quick income? Have you thought of what you really want to do with your life? Are you willing to take a step backward so that you can move two or more steps forward? Are you ready to stop complaining and start doing?

My mind-pattern pulls long-term, satisfying employment to me.

Day Six

Do you avoid release work because you do not want to deal with any unpleasantness that is buried? Are you willing to do release work for long-term peace of body, mind, and soul? Are you willing to start now?

I achieve long-term peace of body, mind, and soul.

Day Seven

Do you look continually to others for answers you could obtain yourself? Are you willing to do the long-term work that it takes to find your own answers? Are you willing to take the time to internally explore Self, Oversoul, and God-Mind to achieve the long-term benefits of self-knowledge?

I achieve the long-term benefits of self-knowledge.

My wise choices bring long-term quality of life.

Loose Ends

Day One

What loose ends need concluding before you can start a new cycle? Do you have unsatisfied desires that need fulfillment so that you can release the old cycle? Conclude your loose ends from the old cycle so that you can begin a new cycle.

I conclude all loose ends from old cycles.

Day Two

If there are foods that you desire but have avoided, eat these foods so you can tie up this loose end. Fulfill the desire so that you remove the weight of it from your mind.

I conclude all food loose ends.

Day Three

If there is anyone that you need to forgive, including yourself, now is the time. Without forgiveness, you leave a lot of loose ends that prevent your progress. Understand your issues and let them go so you can move on.

I conclude all forgiveness loose ends.

Day Four

Is there anyone that you need to visit, but have avoided? Visit the people who need your attention so that you can conclude these loose ends.

I visit others to conclude loose ends.

Day Five

Conclude all unfinished projects. Either finish them, make arrangements for someone else to finish them, or dispose of them. Finish up all these loose ends so that you can move on.

I conclude the loose ends of all unfinished projects.

Day Six

If you need to make any medical, financial, legal, or other appointments, schedule them as soon as possible to finally remove them from your "to do" list.

I conclude the loose ends of all appointments.

Day Seven

Organize and clean out the old to prepare for the new. Dispose of everything no longer necessary; organize all that you need.

I conclude the loose ends of cleaning.

I conclude all loose ends from old cycles.

Magnificence

Day One

Pull the magnificence of your soul-personality to the forefront. Be the bright and shining light that you designed yourself to be. To bring this into physical reality, clean and polish all the bright and shining decorations in your home, yard, and car—chrome, mirrors, and decorations, for example.

The magnificence of my soul-personality shines.

Day Two

Look in the mirror at your reflection. Acknowledge that every cell of your being on all levels is a magnificent creation.

Every cell of my being is magnificent.

Day Three

Looking in the mirror at your reflection, see the sparkling glow of magnificence around your physical body. Relax your eyes. Let them lazily and a bit unfocused float around the perimeter of your physical body. See the glow of magnificence emanating from your physical body. See that glow all day.

I emanate the sparkling glow of magnificence.

Day four

Feel the magnificence that flows through every cell of your being. Visualize a switch at the pineal gland. Mentally turn it on. Feel electrified and alive as the magnificence of God-Mind flows through you.

The magnificence of God-Mind flows through my every cell.

Day Five

Without judgment or criticism, objectively notice how brightly your being shines compared to others around you. Give thanks for the magnificence of your being as well as your ability to consciously experience this.

I give thanks for the magnificence of my being.

Day Six

"A bright light attracts many bugs." This means that on some level, others see and recognize your light. Your light may be too bright for some, for in the magnificence of your light, others see things about themselves that they may not like. Your light may attract others who want to hang on to you so that they can live their life through you. Whatever happens, recognize your responsibility to keep your light shining brightly.

I allow the magnificence of my light to shine brightly.

Day Seven

The magnificence that you feel today is only a small sampling of what is yet to come. Allow the floodgate to open and pour continually great flows of magnificence through you.

The flood of magnificence through my being increases daily.

Every cell of my being is magnificent.

Manifesting Relationships

Day One

Do you focus on your relationships or your "non-relationships"? If you want new, healthy, whole, loving relationships, or heal existing ones, you must arrange your mind-pattern to allow others into your life.

I manifest healthy, whole, loving relationships.

Day Two

If you would like a new love interest, look at the part of yourself that prevents this from happening. Why is that part afraid to allow someone new into your life?

I manifest a new love interest into my life.

Day Three

Do you have issues with your parents or other relatives? You can correct these issues on the Oversoul level. At the same time, correct your own internal issues to manifest positive family relationships.

I manifest positive family relationships.

Day Four

Maybe you would like a new friend – someone with whom you can share ideas, travel, or share life's circumstances.

I manifest new, supportive friendships.

Day Five

Maybe you would like a child. Take a look at the part of yourself that prevents this from happening. Maybe you have not found the appropriate significant other. Maybe you block this in your physical body. What part of you prevents this from happening?

I manifest a child into my life.

Day Six

You can communicate with anyone through the Oversoul level, even those who are no longer in body. Your Oversoul delivers your messages, regardless of the location of the soul-personality. You can manifest this relationship in a way that allows you to continue or complete your relationship, according to your desires.

I manifest relationships with those who are no longer in body.

Day Seven

Recognize that all relationships are reflections of yourself, both positive and negative. Everyone who is in your life (and those who are not) is making statements about your current state of inner being. Learn from this. Keep what you like, and learn from what you do not, so that you may manifest the most perfect relationships for you.

I manifest the most perfect relationships for myself.

I manifest healthy, whole, loving relationships.

Memory

Day One

Did you ever go from one room into the next, only to forget why you went there in the first place? Or, have you ever been distracted during one task, started another task, and then realized that you forgot to finish the first one? A good short-term memory is important to effectively and efficiently get through your day.

My short-term memory is excellent.

Day Two

Have you ever gone shopping, forgotten your list, and come home without everything you need? Do you have any blank spots in your memories over the last few years? Are your childhood memories spotty, scarce, or non-existent?

My long-term memory is excellent.

Day Three

Childhood memories that are long forgotten may be important in your current mental work. There may be gaps in your memory that are important for you to fill in to better understand who you are and where you came from.

I remember all important childhood memories.

Day Four

As your memory improves, you may be surprised at the memories that spontaneously come into your mind. Write these down so that you can piece your unique story together. To build a better memory, glance around your room. Then, close your eyes to mentally recreate your room. Open your eyes to see how well you did. Use this exercise often to strengthen your memory.

I now have a strong memory.

Day Five

Breathe yourself into your center to connect Self, Oversoul, and God-Mind. Within this connection is your inner strength which allows you to observe all memories, even the unpleasant ones. Sometimes, the unpleasant memories are the most important ones as you fill in the gaps. The unpleasant memories may hold keys to understanding the entire puzzle of your life. Learn to be comfortable in uncomfortable situations.

I comfortably observe all unpleasant memories.

Day Six

If you have self-worth issues, you may not allow yourself to have many pleasant memories. Or, you may unrealistically embellish unpleasant memories in a way that turns them into pleasant ones. Learn to realistically recall your memories. This is the only way that you can resolve past experiences.

I realistically recall my memories.

Day Seven

Use your Oversoul to hold your memories. When you need to access your memories, you can accurately retrieve them.

My Oversoul accurately holds my memories.

I now have a strong memory.

Mental Development

Day One

What are you doing with your time? Are you spending excessive amounts of time watching television or on the Internet? Are you involved in mind-numbing activities that hold you where you are or pull you down? Do you usually spend time exploring a wide range of subjects, or do you limit your spare-time activities?

My wise use of time upgrades mental development.

Day Two

Is volunteering a part of your life? If so, is it in balance? Do you use it as a distraction to avoid working on yourself? Do you wear yourself out helping others so that you are too exhausted to help yourself?

I continue my mental development while helping others.

Day Three

Do you include entertainment in your life? Do you control your entertainment, or does your entertainment control you? Is it productive and relaxing, or another stress for you? Does your entertainment elevate or denigrate you?

My entertainment benefits mental development.

Day Four

Are you so focused on "taking care of you" that your life is out of balance? Does "taking care of you" mean the exclusion of other people? Is "taking care of you" turning you into a better person, or a selfish one? Do you care if your words or actions hurt others as long as "you" are okay?

My mental development includes consideration of others.

Day Five

Do you explore family dynamics to aid in your mental development? Do you explore your birth family, extended family, and current family to understand how all these families outpicture your personal, inner family called "you"?

I explore family dynamics to aid mental development.

Day Six

Do you complain, whine, moan, and cry excessively to others about your life circumstances? Is this a healthy way to develop mentally? Do you release your thoughts to your Oversoul so you can grow?

I release my feelings to my Oversoul to increase mental development.

Day Seven

Do you think that you have done so much and made so many changes that there are none left to accomplish? Are you beginning to stagnate amongst your self-admiration? Do you know that good can always get better? Do you keep in mind that God-Mind is endless, and as a microcosm of the macrocosm, so are you?

I identify mental development as an ongoing process.

I explore family dynamics to aid mental development.

Mental Prison

Day One
Have you built a mental prison where there seems to be no way in and no way out? Do you have a mental prison in one area of your life? Or several areas of your life?

I release the need to exist within a mental prison.

Day Two
When everything is going really great, do you feel a need to run back into your mental prison? Do you feel a need to balance high-points of life with self-induced lows? Can you proactively balance your life to maintain an more even emotional flow?

I proactively balance my life to release my mental prison.

Day Three
Are your communication skills locked in a mental prison? Do you want to communicate with others, but you cannot seem to get the words out? Or even if you could, you cannot seem to find anyone with whom to communicate? Do you speak eloquently in private, but cannot get the words out in public?

I release my communication skills from their mental prison.

Day Four
Do you know your personal triggers that push you into an inner mental prison? A place where you automatically go without any conscious direction from anyone? Observe specific triggers that send you scurrying into your own mental prison, so that you can eliminate the need to react in this way.

I identify personal triggers that strengthen mental prisons.

Day Five

Do you withdraw in self-isolation and depression, locked in a mental prison? Why do you choose to experience life this way? Why do you choose to be your own prisoner and guard? Are you ready to release this mind-pattern?

> *I release the mind-patterns that create mental prisons.*

Day Six

Does the outside world play a part in your need to exist within a mental prison? Do you lock yourself away from specific people, places, and/or things? Are you willing to resolve these external issues to gain internal freedom?

> *I gain internal freedom from my mental prison.*

Day Seven

Is the "real you" locked away inside, safe and untouchable by others? Is there a part of you that is afraid of living life? Is it easier to stay safe and guarded rather than extend yourself into vulnerability? Do you lock off the joyous parts of yourself as much as the less desirable parts? Are you ready to live your life to its fullest, recognizing that all experiences ultimately come from your Over-soul and God-Mind for your highest benefit?

> *I release my mental prison to live life to its fullest.*

I release the need to exist within a mental prison.

Mental Strength

Day One

The strongest tool that you have is your mind. Acknowledge the strength of your mind by observing all that you have created, whether you label it chaotic and awful, or organized and wonderful. All your surroundings were created by the strength of your own mind-pattern. As commander of your thoughts, your mind consciously directs the creation of your environment.

My mental strength consciously creates my environment.

Day Two

Challenging events are an opportunity to create stronger mind-patterns. Think about your most challenging experiences and what you learned from them. Did you grow stronger because of the experience? Were you able to navigate other challenging experiences even easier?

My mental strength allows me to accept challenging experiences.

Day Three

Be grateful that the holes in your aura are exposed. Exposure allows you to correct, balance, and plug the holes. Ask your Oversoul to expose these holes to you now before they are outpictured in the outer world.

My mental strength now corrects all internal imbalances.

Day Four

Rather than avoid challenging circumstances, become a mental athlete. Accept each daily challenge with gusto and a feeling of accomplishment. Anchor yourself in the strength of Self, Oversoul, and God-Mind by breathing yourself into your center. Gratefully accept all challenges that come your way.

My mental strength surpasses all challenges.

Day Five

Your mind is the key to building an invincible mind-pattern that nothing can penetrate unless you allow it.

My mental strength creates an invincible mind-pattern.

Day Six

What do you accept that creates negative life circumstances? How do you invite them in? Do you allow others to talk you into being an open receptacle for unpleasant circumstances? Who (or what) is in charge of you?

My mental strength creates an impenetrable mind-pattern.

Day Seven

Realize how much of your mental potential goes untapped. Think about the possibilities of increased mental capacity. How far could you go? What would you accomplish? Bring your mental potential into your reality now.

My mental strength operates at full capacity.

My mental strength operates at full capacity.

Merging

Day One

You have many sub-personalities pulling you in a myriad of directions. This confusion results in difficulty focusing and making balanced decisions. The outer world's constant bombardment divides your attention. Use the brown merger archetype at the pineal gland to move through the distractions into a place of self-integration, focus, and internal cohesion.

I merge my Self into a place of focus and cohesion.

Day Two

Your emotions can easily pull and tear you apart, with many different ones surfacing throughout a single event. For example, you may be happy for a friend who receives a promotion at work, while envious that it was not you; sad because the person will be moving to another department; angry because your boss does not notice your hard work, and so on. Every day, you are pulled and torn by emotions.

My emotions merge into inner clarity.

Day Three

Do you have issues from the recent past that you need to release? Do you hold onto them or do they hold onto you? Do they hold you back because they are waiting for resolution? Do you need to merge these issues with your present so you can learn and move on?

I merge my past with my present.

Day Four

What unresolved childhood incidents need to be merged with your present? How are these childhood incidents replicating in your present? Use the brown merger archetype at the pineal gland as you merge your childhood with your present.

I merge childhood with my present.

Day Five

You have "bleed-throughs" from simultaneous lifelines that influence you now. Bring that information forward for a better, fuller, and richer understanding of your present moment. Use the brown merger archetype at the pineal as you merge influencing simultaneous existences with your present.

My influencing simultaneous existences merge with my present.

Day Six

Your conscious, subconscious, and superconscious minds provide the pathway between Self, Oversoul, and God-Mind.

I merge Self, Oversoul, and God-Mind.

Day Seven

You receive many messages at night on many levels of consciousness. Bring that knowledge forward with you into your waking state. Place a brown merger archetype under your pillow at night while you sleep.

My night learning merges with my day learning.

I merge Self, Oversoul, and God-Mind.

Mind-Control

Day One

While many people are becoming increasingly aware of the mass mind-control that is thrust upon society, some are coming into the realization that they are/have been personally targeted for specific reasons. Most people do not publicly speak about their experiences because they fear repercussions from others. When these experiences are not shared, the experience gains power over you. Is there someone with whom you can share your experiences? If not, get a notebook to record your experiences and thoughts. Acknowledging these experience in some way is the first step to correction and balance.

I acknowledge my strange experiences.

Day Two

Some people hear voices, noises, sounds, tones, and/or buzzing, especially between the waking and sleeping state as they fall asleep, or during the night. These may be satellite transmissions and/or ELF pulses that directly affect the brain, and/or interact with the brain waves during the sleep state. These may even be strong enough to force you out of your body. When this happens, use a pale yellow frequency line to trace the source.

I identify the source of strange voices and noises.

Day Three

If you feel extremely depressed, aggressive, and/or are filled with fear and paranoia, this can be the result of mind-control. Flood your entire being with violet, flushing all that you no longer need up to your Oversoul. Be sure to keep your T-Bar archetype balanced and spin your chakras daily.

I keep myself balanced to counter mind-control effects.

Day Four

If you have been subjected to mind-control, you may find that you easily disassociate yourself from others and the environment. You may feel that you easily flip between personalities, or your moods unexpectedly change. When this happens, use the brown merger archetype at the pineal gland to bring all parts of Self together.

I merge my Self into one.

Day Five

You may notice sudden behavior changes in yourself, others, or even children. These may strike you as odd or unusual. If so, use violet to protect yourself from ELF pulses.

I use violet to protect against mind-control effects.

Day Six

If you have any unusual body markings, moles, or growths that suddenly appear, use castor oil on them to counter the effects. Mentally, flood them with violet.

I neutralize unusual body markings, moles, and/or growths.

Day Seven

Blurred vision, vision changes, or even facial features changing may be a sign of mind-control, as well as "blank faces" and/or vacant stares. Observe when you feel these things occur and write them down.

I keep a journal of my unusual experiences.

I use violet to protect against mind-control effects.

Mission

Day One

There is a reason why you are here. As a multidimensional being, your tasks are layered and multidimensional. Use the strength of your thoughts to become consciously aware of your current mission.

I am consciously aware of my mission.

Day Two

There are many distractions and temptations that attempt to prevent you from accomplishing your mission. Think about what it is that want to accomplish at this time, and focus on accomplishing it. Decide what diverts you from your original, narrow path so that you can immediately correct it.

I focus and concentrate upon my mission.

Day Three

Do you rely more on outside sources than yourself, Oversoul, and God-Mind? Are you doing what you think that you "should" be doing? Are you too influenced by everyone around you? Do others pull you into their dramas that prevent you from taking care of your own life? How do outside sources influence you?

I rely on Self, Oversoul, and God-Mind to direct my personal mission.

Day Four

Do you see cycles within your inner and outer work? Do they come together at any point? When you are in sync with your mission, there is no difference between the outer and inner work—it is the same, no matter where you are, no matter what you do.

My inner and outer work are in sync with my mission.

Day Five

Do you see your career/job as a part of your mission? There is always a thread connecting all aspects of your life. However you spend your time working is a statement of your mission.

My career is a statement of my mission.

Day Six

You may not consciously know all the steps that you need to accomplish your mission. If you take one step at a time, the next step reveals itself. You are fed bits and pieces of your mission on a "need-to-know" basis. When you feel frustrated, remember that all things are in "God's time, not your time." Know that all will be revealed as you are ready.

I accomplish my mission one step at a time.

Day Seven

Release the people who are unaccepting, uncomfortable, and unable to understand your goals and mission in life. Let these people, places, and things go, knowing that everyone and everything that you need now enters your life. Create the support team that you need to bring your mission to fruition.

All areas of my life support my mission.

I am consciously aware of my mission.

Morning Affirmations

Day One

Establishing a morning routine with affirmations personalized for you sets the tone for the entire day. Quickly going through a few affirmations every morning pulls you up into your potential, regardless of how you feel at the moment. Do not stop to judge or criticize; merely use your own words to set your present in motion. Begin by using an affirmation to create your ideal weight.

I am now my ideal weight.

Day Two

While going through your morning grooming routine, appreciate the beauty that permeates all levels of your being. Rather than concentrate on what you may not like about yourself, concentrate on what you do like, adding strength to who and what you are.

Every cell of my being is magnificently beautiful/handsome.

Day Three

As you dress, concentrate on the regeneration process. With your mind, you create your body every day. Know that with your mind, you can rebuild, regenerate, restructure, realign, and renew the physical body.

My body functions at optimum capacity.

Day Four

While making your bed, feel yourself financially free and independent of any mental, emotional, physical, and spiritual encumbrances.

All of my debts are paid; I am financially free and independent.

Day Five

As you eat breakfast, acknowledge the symbolism of the food that you ingest. What does it tell you about your day? Does the food nourish your system or merely fill up an empty stomach?

My day nourishes all levels of my being.

Day Six

While cleaning up from breakfast, affirm your own self-worth, knowing that your day reflects this back to you.

I appreciate all that I am and all that I have to offer.

Day Seven

All challenges are an opportunity to stretch and grow. See yourself strong and flexible like a tree, able to bend and move with the wind without breaking.

I am flexible and open to the growth my day brings.

My body functions at optimum capacity.

Morning Routine

Day One

Establishing a regular morning routine sets the tone for the entire day. When you first wake up, mentally visualize yourself in brown to remember your dreams. Keep a notebook by your bed to keep a written log of your dreams. Even if you can only recall a small bit of the dream, write it down. This opens the process of consciously receiving these messages from yourself.

I remember and understand my dreams.

Day Two

During the night, while the body is resting, you are still active. In the morning, release everything that you learned in the night up to your Oversoul so that your personal cup is ready for a refill!

I release all learning from the night up to my Oversoul.

Day Three

Ask your Oversoul to prepare you for your day and your day for you. This prepares every person, place, and object in a way that all can handle in the most comfortable way.

I am prepared for my day and my day is prepared for me.

Day Four

If you foresee specific issues with specific people, address these via the Oversoul level. Use your morning routine to prepare for the resolution of any issues that can be worked out in advance.

I resolve my day's issues in advance.

Day Five

Balance your T-Bar archetype located at your pineal gland to bring the left and right-brain hemispheres into balance. Check throughout the day to ensure that your T-Bar stays straight. Or, you can visualize the pineal gland archetype at the pineal gland, which is a royal blue circle with a royal blue dot in the middle.

My left and right-brain are in balance.

Day Six

Spin your chakras every morning to ensure that all the colors are in the proper sequence with the correct hue for optimum health.

I spin my chakras for optimum health.

Day Seven

Establish a morning routine that works best for you. Your morning routine does not have to take a lot of time – but create something efficient and easy that works for you on a consistent basis.

My morning routine enriches my day.

I remember and understand my dreams.

Mother

Day One

Everyone has some kind of "mother" issue simply because this is the vehicle through which you enter into this reality. Your mother is the one person who most reflects who you are at the moment of birth. She becomes the primary person who imprints you, either through caring or not caring for you. As your primary caregiver, she becomes your focal point. What kind of relationship did you have with your mother as a child?

> *I accurately assess my childhood relationship with my mother.*

Day Two

As you moved into your teen years and early adulthood, how did your relationship with your mother progress? How did you feel about her at that time? What kind of imprinting did you receive from her during these formative years?

> *I accurately assess my imprinting from my mother.*

Day Three

How is your current relationship with your mother? Or, if she has passed away, what was it at the time of her passing? Does she have the ability to "push your buttons"? Do you accept her for what she is? Do you have a picture in your mind of what you want her to be? Are you disappointed and/or hurt when your mother does not fulfill this picture?

> *I accurately assess my current relationship with my mother.*

Day Four

How has her imprinting affected your relationship with other females? Do you treat females as your mother treated you? Did you feel powerless so you now have a need to in some way overpower or even denigrate females? Did you feel weak so now you need to dominate? Or do you still feel weak and replicate this feeling in your relationships?

I assess the effect of my mother's imprinting on my relationships.

Day Five

Do you feel loved by your mother? Is this okay or not? How does this affect love for Self? How do you extrapolate this onto others? If you do not think your mother loves you, can anyone love you, including Self? Do you feel that your mother did the best that she could under her unique set of circumstances?

I love myself.

Day Six

Do you always seek your mother's approval in one form or another? Does this bring up any rejection issues? If so, how do you extrapolate this onto others? Do you constantly seek approval from others? Do you set up self-sabotage routines so this does not happen? What do you repeatedly recreate around your mother's imprinting that you no longer need?

I approve of myself.

Day Seven

Whether she is in or out of body, explore your mother issues on the Oversoul level. Release your emotional feelings, both positive and negative. Even if you logically understand your mother, you may have an emotional side that needs release and explanation. Resolving these issues frees you to create new imprints that better serve you now.

I resolve my mother issues to free my Self.

I accurately assess my imprinting from my mother.

Needs

Day One
In rough times, many people worry about the future. Knowing that you are consciously connected to your Oversoul helps you realize that all your needs are always met.
All my needs are always met.

Day Two
Many people worry about their financial resources. Give your worries and concerns up to your Oversoul and God-Mind. Know that your financial needs are always met.
My financial needs are always met.

Day Three
You may question your access to a nourishing food supply if times become dire. Know that you have all the nourishing food that you need.
I always have all the food that I need.

Day Four
The strength of your mind-pattern pulls to you everything that you need. No matter where you are or who you are with, or how the outer circumstances appear, it is ultimately your mind-pattern that determines what comes to you.
The strength of my mind-pattern always pulls to me everything that I need.

Day Five

The strength of your mind-pattern determines who is around you and why. No one can be in your space unless there is something that attracts them from within you. Conversely, no one can move out of your space unless there is nothing in your mind-pattern to keep them there. Know that everyone who is supposed to be with you is with you at the appropriate times.

I have all the people around me who I need.

Day Six

Do your housing circumstances concern you? Do you trust your Oversoul and God-Mind to take care of you? Do not put limitations on yourself, your needs, and most importantly how your needs are to be met. Pass your fears and concerns up to your Oversoul and God-Mind, knowing that what you need is with you now. Sometimes, it is darkest before the dawn.

My housing needs are now met.

Day Seven

Transportation needs may be an issue for you. You may have concerns about such things as air travel, fuel prices, and public transportation safety. Know that you are always in the correct place at the correct time.

My transportation needs are met.

All my needs are always met.

New Growth

Day One
Foster new growth within. Plant some seeds in a cup on your windowsill. As the seeds germinate, recognize the symbolism of the seed.

I allow new inner growth.

Day Two
Purchase a flowering plant. What color did you choose? How is the color significant to new inner growth?

I allow my inner growth to bloom.

Day Three
Plant or purchase a small herb garden. Herbs provide balance to your physical body.

My new growth balances my body, mind, and soul.

Day Four
Plant a young tree or bush in your garden. Recognize that new growth comes in all shapes and sizes.

I recognize new growth in the garden of my soul-personality.

Day Five
Plant a pot of strawberries for your windowsill, deck, or yard. Enjoy its flowers and fruit. Recognize that your new inner growth bears fruit in your outer life.

My new inner growth bears fruit in the outer world.

Day Six

Plant tomatoes, recognizing that there are many areas of your inner life that are ready to bear fruit. Positive growth in one area of life means positive growth in other areas.

All areas of my life bear fruit.

Day Seven

Sprout salad seeds, such as mung beans, alfalfa seeds, broccoli seeds, and radish seeds on a wet paper towel or in a sprouting jar. Use these sprouts in a fresh salad with your favorite salad dressing.

I have an abundance of new growth in my life.

I allow new inner growth.

Next Level

Day One

Are you ready to move on, but something holds you back? Do you think you need a little nudge to get you over the hump and into your next level of growth? Do you feel so close, yet so far away? Review the status of your life for trends that continually repeat. Review your career, finances, health, and relationships.

I release repetitive cycles from my life.

Day Two

What kinds of trends did you find in your self-review? How are they related? For example, are you constantly abandoned by people either emotionally or physically, personally or professionally? Do you have a trend of starting ideas, projects, and goals, but never bringing them to completion? Trace these trends to their points of origin. Where did these trends begin?

I find the point of origin of my repetitive cycles.

Day Three

Why do you need to keep these trends? What emotional needs do they fulfill? Do you have a need to punish yourself? Do you have a need to feel "less than"? Do you need an excuse to not let your light shine?

*I release all that prevents moving into my
next level of development.*

Day Four

Energetically, move into your next level of development. Envision your current life as a layer of energy. Feel yourself in that layer of energy. Look up to see the top of that energy layer. Move your consciousness above the current layer of energy. Look down on the layer that you just passed through.

I easily move into my next level of development.

Day Five

Practice functioning in your next level of development. As you go about your daily activities, recognize that you are no longer a part of this energetic layer of experience. Hold your consciousness above this energetic layer of experience. Observe where you were and where you are now.

I easily function in my next level of development.

Day Six

In your new level of awareness, look back at the old energy layer that you passed through. Determine if there is anything trying to pull you back. Look for energetic cords that tie you to people, places, and/or things. Via the Oversoul level, release these energetic cords to their rightful owners.

I fully function in my next level of development.

Day Seven

Whenever you feel tied to the old energetic level, recognize all that it contained. Give thanks for both positive and negative experiences. Then, release all energetic cords. Continue to hold your focus in your new level so strongly that the new layer automatically exists around you. Prepare your space, mentally, physically, emotionally, and spiritually so that everything is in order to exist in the new level of development.

I exist in my new level of development.

I release repetitive cycles from my life.

Opening the Flow

Day One

As your awareness deepens, the amount of your soul-personality expressing in and through you creates a strong energetic flow that you can feel. Visualize a fountain. Stand in the center of that fountain. Feel the limitless flow in every cell of your being.

I feel the deep energetic flow of my soul-personality.

Day Two

Incorporate water as a visual aid whenever you are in the shower or bathtub. Visualize the energetics of Self, Oversoul, and God-Mind flowing effortlessly through you. Feel this connection in every cell of your being.

I am connected to the energetic flow of my
Oversoul and God-Mind.

Day Three

Every time you use water or are near it, remind yourself that the energy of Self, Oversoul, and God-Mind flows freely and effortlessly through every level of your life.

The energy of Self, Oversoul, and God-Mind flows
effortlessly through my life.

Day Four

When you have the opportunity to swim, do so with the awareness that you are in the flow of Self, Oversoul, and God-Mind. You can also visualize swimming in your mind, feeling the support of the flow of Self, Oversoul, and God-Mind. Feel the buoyancy of the flow, lifting and supporting you through all of life's experiences.

The flow of Self, Oversoul, and God-Mind lifts and supports me.

Day Five

Visualize yourself walking in a rain shower, recognizing the symbolic flow of Self, Oversoul, and God-Mind pouring into every cell of your being. All you have to do is open your arms and receive.

I receive the flow of Self, Oversoul, and God-Mind.

Day Six

Leaking faucets symbolize the flow of Self, Oversoul, and God-Mind that pours into you and then right out of you. On some level, you refuse the flow. Fix the leaking faucets in your outer life to fix the leaking faucets of your inner life.

I utilize the flow of Self, Oversoul, and God-Mind.

Day Seven

Exist in the flow of Self, Oversoul, and God-Mind. Everywhere you go, whomever you are with, allow every cell of your being to exist in the flow. Feel the energetic flow strong and full, opening your conscious connection to the trinity within.

I exist in the flow of Self, Oversoul, and God-Mind.

I receive the flow of Self, Oversoul, and God-Mind.

Opportunities

Day One

Many people sit, waiting for the "right" opportunity to happen, wondering why it never shows up. Sometimes what you see as the "right" opportunity is not in alignment with the wishes of your Oversoul and God-Mind. From a higher level all the consequences are known. From your level of reality, you may only see a portion of the consequences. What you view as the "right" opportunity may not be the "correct" one.

I allow my Oversoul and God-Mind to discern correct opportunities.

Day Two

You may at times focus on what you perceive to be lost or missed opportunities. If these were correct opportunities, you would have chosen them. Think of the teachers who were not chosen to be the first teacher/astronaut on the Challenger space shuttle. How many went to bed that night upset? How many were thanking God the next day when the space shuttle exploded?

I release all negative feelings from opportunities perceived as missed.

Day Three

Do you have regrets about what "should have/would have/could have" been? Think about these times, releasing them to your Oversoul and God-Mind as the thoughts come forward into your conscious mind.

I release all my perceptions of "failed" opportunities.

Day Four

There is an old story about a man stranded on top of a house during a flood waiting for God to rescue him. A boat came and then a helicopter, but he refused their services. When he died, he asked God why He had not rescued him. God replied that He sent a boat and helicopter—what more did the man want? Sometimes people have actual opportunities that are sanctioned by their Oversoul and God-Mind, but they fail to recognize them.

I immediately recognize all correct opportunities.

Day Five

What are you looking for in your life? What kind of opportunity do you feel you need? Have you discussed this with your Oversoul and God-Mind? Are you set on one thing, or are you willing to change your idea of a "correct" opportunity? Are you willing to release your feelings of "opportunities gone wrong" to make room for correct ones? Do you still have negative feelings that hold space inside of you?

The strength of my mind-pattern pulls correct opportunities to me.

Day Six

If you are not sure what to do or how to pull an opportunity to you, do you just sit and wait for something to happen? Or, do you proactively search out opportunities? Stagnation means death on all levels. Use your affirmations, and follow through with some physical action to begin to find the correct opportunities. Knock on as many doors as you find, continually thanking your Oversoul for opening the correct one.

I proactively find correct opportunities that move me forward.

Day Seven

Once you find your opportunity, keep your alignment of Self, Oversoul, and God-Mind so that you do not self-sabotage. Know that you deserve all beneficial and correct experiences. Release the need to self-sabotage.

I deserve all correct opportunities that come my way.

I allow new inner growth.

Organization Part I

Day One

Everything in God-Mind is already organized. What appears to be chaos is only organization not yet understood. Understand that your own mind-pattern has a specific order to it, even if that order appears in such a way that you do not understand it yet.

I understand the order of my own mind-pattern.

Day Two

When it is difficult to find order within, the best thing to do is to create order without. The mind-pattern has no choice but to reflect this back. Take a look at your least organized physical space, or a space that bothers you. What does this physical space represent in your life? Choose a small area and start the organization process.

I organize my outer world to organize my inner world.

Day Three

Look for hidden areas to organize—drawers, cabinets, closets, baskets, corners, purses, wallets, etc. These represent unorganized hidden corners of your mind-pattern. Cleaning out and organizing cleans out and organizes some of the information contained within your own mind-pattern.

I organize hidden areas of my outer world to reveal
hidden areas of my inner world.

Day Four

If you visit or work in places that are not organized, this is a reflection of your mind-pattern. You do not live in it, but you must occasionally be in it. What do these places represent? What part of your mind-pattern attracts disorganization to you and why?

My mind-pattern attracts organization.

Day Five

Do others in your life live in disorganization? If so, what part of your mind-pattern do these people reflect? What exists within yourself that allows you to see this within others? Is this your past, present, or future? Do you judge others because of this? What part of your life needs organization from what you observe in others?

I allow others to teach me about organization.

Day Six

If you are "overly" organized, then you may have some control issues. Move your physical world around to gain flexibility in your inner world.

I re-organize my physical world to gain flexibility in my inner world.

Day Seven

There is always a balance within God-Mind and therefore, within you. If you have places where you are "overly" organized, then you have places that are "under" organized. Create a balance within your own mind-pattern to achieve balance on all levels.

I create balance within my organization process.

I understand the order of my own mind-pattern.

Organization Part II

Day One

Organize your finances. Keep your accounts in balance, bills paid in a timely manner, and be aware of your cash flow. Organizing your finances helps you organize the abundance of Oversoul and God-Mind energy available to you.

I organize the abundance of Oversoul and God-Mind energy available to me.

Day Two

Emotions become intertwined with each other. Perhaps you say that you are angry at a friend when you are really angry at yourself. Perhaps you say that you feel love from someone when you really feel control from them. Take some time to understand what you really feel to properly organize your emotions.

I organize my emotions.

Day Three

Organize your spiritual path in a way that makes sense to you. Think about what you are doing and if this is the correct path for you. Think about what you want to do and if your "wants" are the same as your "needs." Discard anything that you hold onto that no longer serves a purpose.

I organize my spiritual path.

Day Four

Organize your projects. Make decisions that allow you to complete your projects in a timely manner. Understand the symbolism of these projects and how each one outpictures your mind-pattern.

I organize my projects to understand their inner symbolism.

Day Five

Organize something that is out in the open; something that you walk past every day, and never even notice any more. Perhaps it is a pile of papers, a corner in your kitchen, or a windowsill that is crowded.

I organize all inner and outer aspects that I have overlooked.

Day Six

Organize your plants and flowers to represent organizing your inner growth. Clean them up, trim off the old, repot, and replace them as needed.

I organize my inner growth.

Day Seven

Organize your jewelry. Untangle necklaces, bracelets, earrings, pins, and watches. Sort them so that you can easily find the piece that you need at the appropriate time. Repair or replace anything that is broken or does not work. Clean away accumulated dirt –soak your gold and silver in distilled water with baking soda overnight so that they sparkle once again.

I organize my inner gems.

I organize my inner growth.

Oversoul Family

Day One

Have you taken time to explore your Oversoul? On the inner level, move your consciousness up into the place above your head that contains your connection to your Oversoul. Ask for your Oversoul to show you whatever it wants in regards to its vastness. What kind of thoughts, pictures, images, feelings come into your mind?

I explore my Oversoul.

Day Two

Put a silver infinity symbol above your head. Move your mind up to your Oversoul level, then ask it to show you how it arranges itself as an extension of God-Mind. Observe your thoughts, pictures, images, and feelings.

I understand how my Oversoul is an extension of God-Mind.

Day Three

Ask your Oversoul to show you itself simultaneously expressing in this and other realities; in this timeline and in others. Observe your thoughts, pictures, images, and feelings. Do not "try" to get anything. Just hold your consciousness above you in your Oversoul level, relax, hold the question at your pineal gland, and see what happens. There is no right or wrong.

I understand the simultaneous expressions of my Oversoul.

Day Four

Ask your Oversoul to bring the necessary members of your Oversoul family together so that you may have company as you explore God-Mind together.

The necessary members of my Oversoul family now come together.

Day Five

Ask your Oversoul to allow members of your Oversoul family to recognize you at the appropriate time. Simply because you recognize them does not mean that they recognize you. Even if they do recognize you, they may have other goals to accomplish that do not include you.

My Oversoul family recognizes me at the appropriate time.

Day Six

Keep in mind that every member of your Oversoul family experiences this reality in his/her own way. For this reason, you may recognize his/her inner frequency, but the outer layers may be layered with experiences that do not match yours. Do preparation work so that when the time comes, everyone positively recognizes each other in a way that is meaningful and conducive to harmony.

I am ready for my Oversoul family and my Oversoul family is ready for me.

Day Seven

Within an Oversoul family, no one is exactly the same. Everyone has a different function, but the whole has the possibility to function in great harmony. Ask that each member of the gathering Oversoul family be prepared to function in harmony.

I move in harmony with my Oversoul family.

I explore my Oversoul.

Panic

Day One

Panic is fear magnified, striking many highly intelligent people in a variety of subtle ways. Sometimes you get so accustomed to panic that you do not even stop to label it as such. If you feel faint or like you are going to vomit, get weak in the knees, heart palpitations increase, and/or your breathing becomes shallow, you may be experiencing the onset of panic.

I release the need for panic.

Day Two

The feeling of panic is often brought on by speaking publicly, either to one person or to a group. This includes speaking up for yourself. Whenever these feelings produce symptoms of panic, allow them to flow up to your Oversoul.

Panic flows out of me and into my Oversoul.

Day Three

Are you the type of person who almost reaches his/her goal, almost brings something positive to completion, almost gets a raise, almost wins, almost gets there, but not quite? Sometimes when a person gets too close to a goal, a part of Self panics because the person is accustomed to self-sabotage. Panic sets in because there is a part of Self that is conditioned not to ever reach the goal.

I move through panic to complete and surpass all goals.

Day Four

Panic can set in when you leave a safe environment. This may be your country, state, city or town, neighborhood, or even your own home or room. Everyone has an environment that is familiar and safe. If you feel panic whenever you are outside of your safe place, move through the panic a step at a time. If leaving your room is difficult, do not plan to travel outside your area of familiarity. Move from your room to the rest of the house. From the house, stand outside the house, and so forth. Slowly, a step at a time until panic no longer controls where you go.

I move through panic to feel safe wherever I am,
whatever my environment.

Day Five
Some people panic when they are in enclosed in small places. If this happens to you, breathe in medium green from your Oversoul to oxygenate the entire body. Allow the body to take control so that it can breathe when your mind closes from the panic. Your body automatically knows how to breathe itself if you let it. When you are in a wide open space, put these panic memories at the pineal gland to determine what brought about the initial feelings of panic.

I oxygenate with medium green to easily move through panic.

Day Six
Sometimes, the feeling that you are not in control leads to feelings of panic. This could be anything from relationships to public transportation. Realize that your Oversoul is always in control. Whatever happens is always for your highest good.

I replace panic with Oversoul guidance.

Day Seven
Focus on other things that create feelings of panic. These might include anything from animals to specific sounds or smells to being alone. Allow whatever causes panic to come into your conscious mind while you are in a safe environment so that you can easily deal with it. In this way, you can control panic before panic controls you.

I proactively deal with panic.

I release the need for panic.

Personal Frequencies

Day One

Specific types of people have a common frequency. For example, all mothers have a common frequency. Think of everyone you know who is a mother. Feel the common frequency.

I identify the mother frequency.

Day Two

All fathers have a common frequency. Think of everyone you know who is a father. Feel the common frequency. Now feel the difference between a father frequency and mother frequency.

I identify the father frequency.

Day Three

Siblings have a common frequency. Think of everyone you know who is a brother. Feel the common frequency. Now think of everyone you know who is a sister. Feel that common frequency. Move your consciousness to the father frequency and mother frequency. Feel the sameness of one frequency as well as the differences between frequencies. As you say the following affirmation, feel the frequency change when you go from the word "brother" to the word "sister."

I identify brother and sister frequencies.

Day Four

All family relationships have specific frequencies. Husbands and wives have specific frequencies, as well as sons and daughters, grandmothers and grandfathers, aunts and uncles, nieces and nephews. As you read, identify the specific frequency of each familial group. Identify the sameness and difference between the frequencies.

I identify family frequencies.

Day Five

The frequency of friend has a different frequency than that of an enemy. What does a "friend" frequency feel like?

I identify the frequency of friendship.

Day Six

How about co-workers and colleagues? How does that kind of frequency feel? Explore this group to determine its frequency.

I feel and know the frequency of co-workers and colleagues.

Day Seven

Practice identifying frequencies. Whenever you come in contact with someone, go to the Oversoul level to determine which frequency the person is on. He/she may be on more than one— such as mother, sister, aunt, wife, friend, and so forth.

I identify the frequencies of all people.

I identify family frequencies.

Personal Time

Day One

Because the days fill up so quickly, you may not be taking any time to take care of yourself. It is important to spend some time on yourself so that who you are does not get lost in the daily process of life. You can use many excuses not to take care of yourself, but the bottom line is that this reflects a mind-pattern of low self-worth.

I use personal time to increase self-worth.

Day Two

When you do not take the time to take care of yourself, you re-emphasize mind-patterns of self-sabotage and self-abuse. Today, take five minutes to do some gentle stretching exercises to release internal and external tensions and stresses. Move, stretch, bend, and be good to yourself.

I use personal time to move through self-sabotage and self-abuse.

Day Three

You may have a mind-pattern of not being "good enough." This means that you do not allow yourself the inner freedom to spend time on yourself. What do you do for others? Do you do the same for yourself?

I use personal time to do something special for myself.

Day Four

You may not allow personal time because there are inner issues that you wish to avoid. Keeping yourself defocused means you do not have to deal with inner thoughts and feelings. Denying yourself personal time may stem from a mind-pattern of fear of facing yourself and/or your life. Take a quiet walk, sit in your favorite chair in your favorite room sipping a cup of tea, or go to a peaceful outdoor area to relax and think.

I use personal time to face my inner Self.

Day Five

Make an appointment for a wellness activity; something that refreshes and nurtures body, mind, and soul. Consider a massage, pedicure, manicure, facial, body wrap, or even a chiropractic adjustment. Think about bringing a meal in instead of cooking, or cooking for yourself instead of bringing a meal in. Be creative.

I use personal time to nurture body, mind, and soul.

Day Six

Let someone do something for you. Whenever anyone offers, gracefully accept the offer. If they do not offer, then suggest. If they hesitate, insist upon it. Let others know that you would like someone to help you, just as you help others.

I allow others to help me during my personal time.

Day Seven

Choose one day a week to do something to honor your own uniqueness. The activity does not need to be long and involved. The activity only needs to be long enough for you to stop to acknowledge Self.

I use personal time to honor my own uniqueness.

I use personal time to face my inner Self.

Physical Body

Day One

Rather than tell your body what you are going to do to it, ask your body what it wants done However, do not let your body control the process. Form a team with the same goals of wellness and beauty.

I work as a team with my physical body.

Day Two

Recognize that whatever your body is, it is a product of your own creative thinking process. Know that your body is a statement about who and what you are up to this point in linear time and space. Your body is a visual representation of your current mind-pattern. This means that by interpreting your body, you can better understand your current mind-pattern.

I know my body; I know my mind-pattern.

Day Three

Look in the mirror every chance you get. Realize that positive statements about your body create a beautiful body. Negative statements pull away the life force from the body part that you are denigrating. Visualize and feel the body that you would like to create. Now, create it!

My body is magnificently beautiful!

Day Four

If you think that your body weighs too much, realize that you are insulating against life. Think about any situations that you have suppressed into your body. Give them to your Oversoul and God.

My body is at its perfect weight.

Day Five

Forget about dieting. Instead, work on cleaning out your physical body so that it can hold more soul energy. Allow your physical body to feel empty so that you can fill it up with something else. Stop stepping on the scales in a self-defeating ritual. Decide in your mind what you would like to weigh, then hold that thought as the cleaning begins. Cleaning out the physical body represents cleaning out the mind.

I clean out my physical body to clean out my mind.

Day Six

Even the healthiest bodies can become healthier. Rather than focus on any individual area, feel the healing flow of God-Mind permeating each and every cell of your being. Give the healing flow color, weight, and consistency. Feel it, know it, be it.

The healing flow of God-Mind permeates every cell of my being.

Day Seven

Your physical body totally regenerates itself once every seven years. So, why does a person age? Release the weight of your experiences up to your Oversoul—watch them flow out the top of your head. Give the flow color, weight, and consistency. When you do this, you actually move excess energy out of your auric field. Your body becomes lighter, stronger, and more youthful.

My physical body is strong and youthful.

My body is magnificently beautiful!

Power Source

Day One

Everyone is connected to an infinite power Source. Visualize your power source shaped like a funnel, from the top of your head on up into infinity. Label the top part "God-Mind." Label the space beneath that "Oversoul." Feel the vastness of your infinite power source.

I feel the vastness of my infinite power Source.

Day Two

To utilize your power Source, your physical structure, meaning your body, must be strong enough to hold great power. What can you do to create a strong physical structure? What kinds of food and supplements do you feed your body? Is your body well-exercised?

My strong physical structure holds great power.

Day Three

Your power Source not only fills your physical structure, it also fills your energetic structure, meaning your auric field. What takes up space in your auric field that is ready to be released? Release all that you no longer need, replacing it with power from your Source.

My energetic structure is filled by my power Source.

Day Four

Visualize your power Source pouring into your physical and energetic structures. Feel the energy flow from your power Source in and through every cell of your being.

The energy from my power Source pours into every cell of my being.

Day Five

Feel your power Source wash, cleanse, clear, strengthen, animate, and activate all of you that exists in this reality. Allow your physical and energetic structures to be filled with as much power from your Source as you can comfortably hold.

I am filled with as much power from my Source as
I can comfortably hold.

Day Six

Feel your internal strength increase and multiply exponentially as you adjust to your conscious connection to your power Source.

My strength multiplies as I consciously connect
to my power Source.

Day Seven

Continually and consciously strengthen your physical and energetic structures to comfortably hold increasingly more power from your Source. Recognize that you, your Oversoul, and God-Mind are now in perfect alignment.

I maintain perfect alignment with my power Source.

My strong physical structure holds great power.

Prepare Your Path

Day One

What are you preparing for? Are you saying one thing but preparing for something else? Do you hope that you do not get any company in the evening because you are tired, yet you hurry around, straightening and cleaning just in case? Do you want health, but stock up on cold remedies and other illness-preventing medications? For what are you preparing?

I prepare for the fulfillment of my desires.

Day Two

Do you say affirmations for abundance of wealth, yet prepare for the opposite? Rather than think about what you do not have, focus on what you do have. Purchase something that makes you feel like you have all the funds in the world. Prepare for the flow!

I prepare for abundance of wealth.

Day Three

Are you looking for a relationship and/or a family, yet you prepare for a life alone? Look around yourself. What represents a life alone and what represents a life with a relationship and family? What do you want? What are you preparing for?

I prepare for a significant relationship.

Day Four

Do you want to take a vacation to a lovely ocean beach? Prepare for it to happen. Get yourself some sunscreen, beach clothes, and towels, and everything that you can think of that you will need. Hold that vision at your pineal gland. Continue to prepare. Set a date of travel. Now, allow it to manifest.

I prepare for the perfect vacation.

Day Five

Do you want to move? Start preparing. Clean out your closets and all old accumulated possessions that you would not move into your new house. Clean up the house to make it ready for sale. Prepare for the sale. Hold that vision at your pineal gland. Allow it to manifest.

I prepare for the sale of my home.

Day Six

It is easy to prepare for what you really desire once you recognize how your actions can contradict your thoughts and words. Align your thoughts, words, and actions to prepare the way for positive experiences to easily enter your life.

I align my thoughts, words, and actions to prepare
for positive experiences.

Day Seven

Become conscious of what you are preparing for. If you do not want something to happen, do not prepare for it. Change the course of life events by changing the course of simple daily actions. Prepare for what you want in accordance with the wishes of your Oversoul and God-Mind within.

I consciously prepare for experiences of my choosing.

I prepare for the fulfillment of my desires.

Proactive

Day One

Most people are prone to be reactive. This means that most people wait until something happens to force them into action. A reactive lifestyle does not allow you much control. Proactive is the opposite. You see a situation and you approach it before it approaches you. This takes a little time and effort, but the end result is that you control your life instead of your life controlling you.

I am proactive in my life.

Day Two

Look around your home or workplace to determine what needs to be cleaned up. Maybe a stack of paper needs filing, a bill needs to be paid, or a refrigerator needs cleaning. Whatever it is, these little "bothers" eat away at you on the inner levels. Quit procrastinating, and today, do something, no matter how small to stop the control that these things have over you.

I am proactive in my environment.

Day Three

Do you have an issue in a relationship that bothers you? Why do you avoid facing this issue? Make an effort to embrace it. Walk up to the person and address the issue as tactfully as possible. Yes, you might have a confrontation, but approaching the situation sooner rather than later lessens the final impact on you both. The longer a situation builds, the more explosive it becomes.

I am proactive in my relationships.

Day Four

How about your work? If you are not satisfied, then it is time to learn to love it so you can let it go. In the mean time, move forward with your innermost plans and desires. Rather than spend your time doing something that you do not like, take action, whatever that may be. Remember, it is your mind-pattern that creates your environment, including your workplace, regardless of what or where it is. You are the creator of your environment - so, create!!

I am proactive in my work.

Day Five

Perhaps you have some personal issues that you are avoiding. These might be leftover from childhood or your school years. These issues can hold you back. You must clean up the past before you can enjoy your present and move into your future. If you do not address these issues, these issues will find ways to address you, sooner or later.

I am proactive in my personal issues.

Day Six

How is your health? Do you have a few extra pounds to lose? Do you need to add a little more physical exercise into your schedule? Do you take a quality multi-vitamin every day? Do you need to see your dentist for a checkup? Do you have any health issues that you are avoiding? Take action today - do something!

I am proactive in my healthcare.

Day Seven

Being proactive means taking control of your life. Being proactive means greeting life's lessons in the least painful, least uncomfortable, least objectionable way. The more lessons you move through in this way, the faster you accelerate your personal learning process. In doing so, you strengthen your mind-pattern. Keep an eye on your life. Seek out that which you have previously avoided. Learn from it so you can move on into bigger and better areas of growth and knowledge.

I am proactive in all facets of my life.

I am proactive in my life.

Programming

Day One

Nightmares and dreams often reveal specific programming codes as they sometimes come to the surface during the dream state. Record these in a journal as the patterns may eventually reveal themselves to you.

I remember and record all significant dreams.

Day Two

Obsessive-compulsive behavior may be the result of specific programming. If this is a factor in your life, trace this back to the time period that this began. Look at the memories that surface.

I identify the origins of undesired, controlling behavior.

Day Three

Some people turn to drugs and/or drinking to deaden the pain of programming experiences that they cannot face. Trace these pain-deadening behaviors back to the time period that they began. Explore that time period. Whenever something traumatic surfaces that you cannot emotionally handle, take a break from your mental exploration.

I bravely face all unpleasant memories.

Day Four

If you cannot remember your childhood, or details are sketchy, there is a good chance that some sort of programming occurred that you are blocking out. Lack of childhood memories is a strong indicator of severe childhood trauma. To unlock closed memories, immerse yourself in dark green. Focus on what you can remember. Explore your memories, recording them in a journal for future consideration.

I unlock all pertinent childhood memories.

Day Five
Program codes are sometimes present in "doodles" that you draw. If you have something that you constantly draw or see, there may be more to it than meets the conscious eye. Draw these down in your journal and study them. Mentally put them in pale yellow to see what knowledge you absorb from them.

I pay attention to all unconscious information.

Day Six
Programmed people have specific triggers that activate them into specific modes of behavior. Whenever a specific behavior happens, realize that something happened to create that. Write down what happened just before these changes occurred. Eventually, you may be able to identify your specific triggers, thus gaining more conscious control of your behavior.

I identify my specific triggers.

Day Seven
Continue to keep your mind and body protected using balancing, protecting, and merging techniques. Use your internal exploration and knowledge of self-awareness to deactivate your personal programs so that you have more control than they have. Keep a journal of all activity so that you can literally piece your personal story together. These notes deepen your self-understanding with ease.

I deactivate outside programming.

I pay attention to all unconscious information.

Progress

Day One

Throughout all your hard work on your inner world, do you take the time to evaluate your progress? Think about what you know today versus what you knew a year ago. What has changed for the better?

I identify my inner progress.

Day Two

How do you feel about yourself, and who and what you are? Are you willing to look at both your positive and negative qualities? Do you find an inner appreciation for the richness that both types of experiences add to your understanding of Self? Progress allows for both sides of the coin to exist with understanding.

I appreciate all qualities of my inner Self.

Day Three

Can you look around and appreciate all that you created? If you see negative creations, can you appreciate the power of your mind? If you see positive creations, can you understand that this is only the beginning? Progress allows you to identify the strength of your own mind-pattern.

I identify the strength of my mind-pattern.

Day Four

Are you gaining understanding for how your outer world reflects your inner world? Are you able to interpret these reflections of Self?

I identify and interpret the outer reflections of my inner progress.

Day Five
Are you actively implementing simple steps to growth, i.e., if you want change, you start with small changes; if you want clarity, you clean your environment, etc.

I know how to change my outer world to create inner change.

Day Six
Are you developing more compassion and understanding for Self and your journey? Are you realizing what a fascinating person you really are? Are you beginning to realize the depth of your own personal journey?

I compassionately understand and appreciate my own inner journey.

Day Seven
Do you judge and criticize Self less? Are you more objective in your observations of Self and others? Do you look at the outer world from the Oversoul level? Do you objectively observe what you, and others, need as opposed to what you want?

I objectively observe Self without judgment and/or criticism.

I identify my inner progress.

Protection

Day One
Notice how far your auric field extends from your body. Visualize a bubble around it.

I create protection with my thoughts.

Day Two
Fill the interior of your bubble with the color violet. Create a mirrored surface on the outside of the bubble.

I am safe and protected.

Day Three
Visualize any inappropriate psychic cords that extend from any person, place, or thing to you. Observe these cords as they fall away, returning to their source via the involved Oversouls.

I protect myself from the control of others.

Day Four
Visualize any inappropriate psychic cords that extend from you to any person, place, or thing. Observe these cords as they fall away, returning to their source via the involved Oversouls.

I protect myself from inappropriately controlling others.

Day Five
Create a mirrored bubble around your home environment, extending it beneath your home as well as above and to all sides. Fill it with the color violet. Place a mirror on the outside of the bubble.

My home is safe and protected.

240 Daily Affirmations for Self-Change

Day Six

All the people that come into your home leave an energetic imprint in it. Everything that you bring into your home contains the energetic imprints of anyone who has touched it. Visualize all the inappropriate energetic imprints returning to their sources via the involved Oversouls. Watch them flow and flow until your home is clean and clear.

My environment is protected.

Day Seven

Create a mirrored bubble around your mode of transportation. Fill it with violet with a mirror on the outside.

I am always protected on my journey through life.

I create protection with my thoughts.

Purpose

Day One

Everyone wants to know his/her purpose. The good news is that you already know. The better news is that you can bring that knowledge to the surface with a few simple exercises and techniques. Start by understanding your surface layers. What is your purpose for today? What necessary functions will you perform? Who is dependent upon you and why?

I know and accomplish my purpose for today.

Day Two

What is your current purpose up to this point in time? Is it being a spouse and/or parent? Does it have to do with employment? What is your motivation to get you up and going in your outer life? Who have you affected and how?

I know and accomplish the purpose for my outer life.

Day Three

How do you feel about your outer life purpose? Did you accomplish that purpose? Are you where you think you ought to be? If you have any outer garments that no longer serve their purpose, are worn out, do not fit, or you no longer wear, throw them out or give them away. Only keep the outer garments that make you feel good about yourself. These represent your outer purpose in life.

I am satisfied with the purpose for my outer life.

Day Four

What is your current inner purpose? To meditate more, eat healthier, lose extra weight, read a book, write, be closer to nature, walk? Do you consider this "busy work" while you wait to find your "real" purpose?

I know and accomplish the purpose for my inner life.

Day Five

What thoughts and feelings lay beneath your current inner purpose? Do you have an ache and an emptiness that is waiting to be filled? Do you keep looking to the outer world thinking that one day you will stumble upon your inner purpose? Are you waiting for someone or something to designate your "true purpose" that will finally allow you to define yourself?

I am satisfied with the purpose for my inner life.

Day Six

Drive your energy down into the next layer, the one that lies beneath the aches and emptiness. Feel the connection of this layer to your subconscious and superconscious minds. Feel that this layer is rich with inner level information. Feel that information flow up through the layers until it reaches the surface of your conscious mind. If you have any inner garments that no longer serve their purpose, discard them as an outer representation of your inner work.

I drive my energy inward to understand my deeper purpose.

Day Seven

Drive your energy down even further, through your subconscious and superconscious minds, deep into your Oversoul and God-Mind. Feel the exchange. Give thanks that your true purpose emerges from the depths of your soul in a way that you can handle. Understand that as you prepare, step by step, you consciously know.

I know and accomplish my deepest purpose.

I know and accomplish my purpose for today.

Rebuilding

Day One
Be sure that your bubble is all around your aura. Breathe all that you no longer need out the top of your head up to your Oversoul. Notice that it is dark and heavy. Breathe in from your Oversoul through the top of your head all that you now need. Notice that it is light and airy.

I breathe out the "bad" and I breathe in the "good."

Day Two
Buy yourself some flowers and/or plants at your local super-market.

I nurture new inner growth.

Day Three
Make a list of the qualities that you like about yourself.

I like myself and all that I am.

Day Four
Rearrange some furniture.

I rearrange my view of my life.

Day Five
Speak, write, phone, email, or visit someone that you have either procrastinated about or avoided.

My inner communication improves.

Day Six
Try a new kind of food, or a new combination of foods that you like.

I willingly take in new, useful mind-patterns.

Day Seven

Go somewhere new.

> *I comfortably travel into new mind-patterns.*

I nurture new inner growth.

Receiving

Day One

Think about all the people who have given to you over the years. Think about the physical gifts you have received. Think about why you attracted those specific items, whether you liked them or not. Decide what these gifts symbolize in your life.

I gratefully receive and understand all that I have manifested.

Day Two

Think about all the nonphysical gifts you have received through the years. Think about why you attracted these nonphysical gifts, whether you liked them or not. Decide what these gifts symbolize in your life, and how they are reflections of you.

I gratefully receive all reflections of myself.

Day Three

If you still have any physical items that you really do not care for, get rid of them. If you are holding onto any nonphysical "gifts" that you no longer need, get rid of them as well.

I create space to receive the new.

Day Four

Make a list of all physical and nonphysical gifts that you would like to receive. Do not label the source; simply know that God-Mind matches the outer world to your inner world.

I graciously and joyously receive all gifts from God-Mind.

Day Five

Feel the flow of perfection through your body, mind, and soul. Give the flow shape, color, form, consistency, and tone.

I receive the perfection of God-Mind in my body, mind, and soul.

Day Six

Know that as a participant in God-Mind, you are open and receptive to all the wonderful aspects of this reality that exist. You are part of the creative flow.

I receive the wonderful aspects of this reality.

Day Seven

Allow yourself to gratefully and joyously receive all that each day offers. Allow yourself to receive all that each person with whom you come into contact offers. All that you receive is a reflection of yourself.

I give thanks for all that I receive.

I give thanks for all that I receive.

Reflection

Day One
Clean the mirrors in your home.
I see the reflections in my life clearly.

Day Two
Make a list of the people in your life who annoy and/or irritate you.
Everything in the outer world is only a reflection of me.

Day Three
Make a list of the people in your life that you enjoy the most.
Everything in the outer world reflects my inner state of being.

Day Four
Make a list of the people in your life with qualities that you admire and would like to cultivate.
Everything in the outer world is a reflection of my potential.

Day Five
Observe the environments in which you live and work.
My environments are reflections of my mind-pattern.

Day Six
What is the weather like today? Are you out in it? Are you protected from it?
The weather reflects the path of my journey.

Day Seven
Clean the mirrors in your home.
I see the reflections in my life clearly.

Everything in the outer world is only a reflection of me.

Regeneration

Day One
Your body is designed for regeneration—even conventional science says that your body totally replaces itself every seven years. So, why does your body deteriorate? What mind-patterns do you carry that substantiate this theory? How is this theory instilled in you throughout the years?
My physical body regenerates.

Day Two
Do you believe that one day you will become old and feeble? Do you hope that someone will be around to take care of you? What kind of self-deprecating mind-pattern is this? Remember that everything is comprised of the same molecules and atoms, it is their arrangement that determines whether you have water, ice, gas, or steam. The same is true for your body. You have the mental power to rearrange the molecular structure of your own body.
My mind regenerates the molecular structure of my body.

Day Three
Focus on everything positive about your body that you can possibly find. Realize that with the strength of your mind, you can recreate and regenerate anything that you consider a body negative.
My mind regenerates my body according to my desires.

Day Four
Use castor oil on any facial lines, scars, skin lesions that need rejuvenation and/or healing. Set a biological age to which you would like your physical body regenerated. Hold that age in your mind-pattern.
My body regenerates and radiates youth, health, and vitality.

Day Five

In your mind, consciously resculpt and recreate your physical body. Give it shape, form, tone, and consistency. Hold that vision in your mind-pattern. Re-direct any negative body thoughts into your new mission of resculpting and recreating a more youthful physical structure. Allow the strength of your focus to recreate a new, strong mind-pattern that has no choice but to bring that vision into physical reality.

The strength of my mind-pattern regenerates my body.

Day Six

Mentally focus on the ideal weight for your physical body, regenerating it inside and out so that the cellular structure is strong, healthy, durable, and flexible. Release the need to step on a scale. Simply continue to focus on sculpting and regenerating the physical body within your own mind-pattern.

My body is at its ideal weight.

Day Seven

Mentally converse with your physical body to determine what regenerative mental and physical foods it needs. This may change from day to day, so while you are actively working on the regenerative process, take a few moments to check in with your physical body every day.

I work with my body to address its needs for regeneration.

My physical body regenerates.

Rejuvenation

Day One
Your auric field is full of vibratory imprints. These imprints have weight, color, tone, and consistency. You put these imprints on one by one, piece by piece. You are so accustomed to carrying them that you do not realize that they are there. In the same way, if you added an ounce of physical weight every day, you would not notice. Eventually, you would be carrying several pounds, but because of its gradual loading you would grow accustomed to the weight. So it is with the vibratory imprints that you carry in your aura. Release these excess energetic imprints up to your Oversoul.

I release excess vibratory imprints to rejuvenate my being.

Day Two
Feel your body, mind, and soul become lighter, cleaner, freer as these imprints leave. You may even feel empty without the weight. To replace your lost weight, breathe in medium green from your Oversoul to oxygenate and rejuvenate your entire system, including your aura.

I breathe in medium green to rejuvenate my body, mind, and soul.

Day Three
Take a look at your cellular structure. Move your consciousness in and through all parts of your body, from head to toe. Look at all the dark, heavy debris that has accumulated. With your mind, watch it fall away, and send it up to your Oversoul. Fill the empty spaces with medium green to lighten and quicken the cellular structure.

My cellular structure rejuvenates as it lightens and quickens.

Day Four

Pay attention to the physical food that you ingest. Do the foods lighten the body and strengthen the framework?

I nourish my body with rejuvenating foods.

Day Five

Do you have a busy lifestyle that does not allow for enough hours of sleep? Tell your Oversoul that you do not mind working if this is what it wants for you, but in exchange, your Oversoul must provide extra energy for the day.

My cellular structure is rested and rejuvenated.

Day Six

Feel your body, mind, and soul vibrate at a new, rejuvenating frequency.

My body, mind, and soul vibrate with a rejuvenating frequency.

Day Seven

Allow body, mind, and soul rejuvenation to continue as an ongoing process. Continue to lighten your load through thought, word, and action. Be good to your body. Incorporate some stretching exercises to pop tensions right out of your muscles. Take in carefully selected mental food to feed your mind. Feed your soul in ways that only you know how. Pay attention to what ages you. Pay attention to what does not. Choose wisely, and all parts of you benefit.

My body, mind, and soul continually rejuvenate.

My body, mind, and soul continually rejuvenate.

Relationship Endings

Day One

Sometimes no matter what you do, you run into a brick wall. You do all your Oversoul level work, you are proactive and greet the situation, yet the person with whom you are interacting absolutely does not budge. You cannot seem to find a compromise unless you compromise your integrity. On the Oversoul level, take a look at the situation to see if you have left no stone unturned.

My Oversoul directs my relationships.

Day Two

If you have successfully tried every avenue that you know of without any give on the other person's part, then sometimes it is time to acknowledge the end of the relationship, whatever that might be. Ask your Oversoul to clearly show you if it is time that your path take you in another direction.

My Oversoul clearly shows me relationship endings.

Day Three

When you are in your center and someone constantly attacks and/or belittles you, then it is time to pick yourself up and leave. Work through this on the Oversoul level first. When you complete this mental process, then physically remove yourself from the relationship.

I end all victim-mentality relationships.

Day Four

When you leave a relationship, evaluate yourself so that you do not re-enter the same type of relationship. Review the mind-pattern that brought this relationship to you in the first place. Think about your mind-pattern at the beginning of the relationship to the present time. Evaluate your changes.

I evaluate myself from the beginning to the end of relationships.

Day Five

There is a fine line between running away from a relationship and leaving because you have truly learned all that is possible from the situation. Review your reasons for leaving to confirm that you are not running away from something, but instead, moving toward something better.

I end relationships to move toward better ones.

Day Six

If another person clearly only wants a relationship on his/her terms, then this is a sign that the relationship needs to be re-evaluated. Are you better off with or without the relationship? Sometimes a relationship is with an organization, a company, a group of people, a pet, a home, a possession. Perhaps you need to evaluate if your goals were ever in alignment with the relationship. Sometimes you find out that what you think is one thing, is really another.

I end relationships that are not in alignment with my highest good.

Day Seven

Ending a relationship may appear to be a lose/lose situation. Expect a certain amount of grieving. You may even feel depressed. Realize that there is a process of letting go.

I end all relationships cleanly and clearly.

I end relationships to move toward better ones.

Releasing

Day One
Dust your home, office, and car.
I release fear from the corners of my mind-pattern.

Day Two
Clean the windows in your home, office, and car.
I release everything that blocks my inner vision.

Day Three
Get rid of old pens or pencils.
I release old ways of communication.

Day Four
Clean your oven.
I release old angers.

Day Five
Throw out any dead plants; trim the ones you have.
I release old stagnant mind-patterns.

Day Six
Throw out old papers and magazines. Sort through any paper piles
that you have accumulated.
I release the clutter of my mind.

Day Seven
Clean out a drawer or a closet; delete some old computer programs
or files.
I release old, buried mind-patterns.

I release my positive experiences to my Oversoul.

Releasing The Positive

Day One
People sometimes forget that good can get better. When life has significantly improved, people are afraid to let it go. A part of you may fear that you will not receive anything better. People are afraid to risk the known for the unknown.

I release the good to get better.

Day Two
Release the energy of positive experiences up to your Oversoul to attract even better experiences into your life.

I release my positive experiences to my Oversoul.

Day Three
Think of some of the positive highlights of the past. Give thanks to your Oversoul and God-Mind for bringing these experiences into your life. Now let them go so that good can get better.

I release the positive highlights of my past.

Day Four
Take a look at your energetic field. Notice all the beautiful, positive energy that exists within it. Release this up to your Oversoul so that your Oversoul can fill you with even more beautiful, positive energy.

I release my positive energy to receive more.

Day Five
Think of some of your favorite jokes or anecdotes that you particularly enjoy telling. Share them with your friends and family today. Then, release this positive energy up to your Oversoul so that more humor and levity can enter your life.

I release humor and levity to receive more.

Day Six

Review some of the unexpected little kindnesses that have come your way from others. Review the little things that you have done for others, both acknowledged and unacknowledged. These simple pleasures were not necessarily highlights of your life, but added to the overall quality. Release the energy of these experiences to make room for more.

I release little kindnesses to receive more.

Day Seven

Visualize the things that bring you pleasure in your life. In your mind's eye, make them better, however that may be. Release your creations up to your Oversoul, and give thanks that it is done. Consistently release your positive experiences to consistently improve your life.

I consistently release my positive experiences to improve my life.

I release my positive experiences to my Oversoul.

Responsibility

Day One

What responsibilities have you assumed and then abruptly left? What has happened in your life where you have tried to make others responsible for decisions that were ultimately yours?

I take responsibility for all my decisions.

Day Two

You have a responsibility to your family. Running away and leaving them behind does not change the fact that you asked to be born into a specific family for specific reasons. If you cannot speak to your family in person, use the Oversoul level. As long as they are in your life in any way, they are a reflection of some part of your past, present, and/or future. You have a responsibility to determine why you chose these people as your family. Similarly, changing your birth name is another form of running away from your family and who you were born to be.

I accept my family responsibilities.

Day Three

You have a responsibility within your chosen work. Whether you like it or not; whether you think someone chose it for you or not, the ultimate decision to follow this path was yours. When you start something you have a responsibility to finish it. If you do not like your chosen work, then you have a responsibility to determine why you are in it. If you cannot finish it, then you have a responsibility to bring it to a conclusion with which all involved can accept.

I accept responsibility for my chosen work.

Day Four

You have a responsibility to maintain your physical surroundings. Your surroundings are a reflection of you. Look around—do you like what you see? If not, you have a responsibility to create something that you do like. Look at your surroundings as if you are seeing them for the first time. How do they look now? How do they look to others seeing them for the first time? What would others have to say about your mental and emotional state based upon what they see?

I have a responsibility to maintain my physical surroundings.

Day Five

You have a responsibility to maintain your physical body. Look at your physical body. What do you see and how do you interpret it? What parts do you like and why? What do these parts state about your mental and emotional state? What parts would you like to change and why? What do these parts state about your mental and emotional state? You have a responsibility to listen to your body and maintain it in accordance with its wishes in alignment with Self, your Oversoul and God-Mind.

I have a responsibility to maintain my physical body.

Day Six

You have a responsibility to the group-mind. Your thoughts, actions, and decisions ultimately affect everything in existence. Are you pleased with what you put out into the collective mind-pattern? Do you uplift it or pull it down?

I have a responsibility to uplift and elevate the group-mind.

Day Seven

You have a responsibility to be an active participant in this life process on Planet Earth. If you were supposed to be someone else or somewhere else, you would be there. You are here to be present at this moment in time. Take responsibility and be present. Stop living in the past or in the future. Take responsibility for your present moment. Live it in the best way that you know how.

I have a responsibility to be in the present moment.

I take responsibility for all my decisions.

Restrictions

Day One

Do you feel that your personal growth is restricted? Do you feel that no matter which way you try to move, doors close rather than open? Look around your home, office, and environment to see what is outpicturing your inner restrictions: a plant with bound roots; clothing that is too tight; anything that is too big or tightly crammed into its space. Remove the physical object from its restricted space.

I remove all restrictions in my life.

Day Two

Do you feel that your creativity is restricted at home or work? Who or what manifests this restricting self-reflection in the outer world? How does this reflect you? What part of yourself chooses to restrict your creativity and why? Enhance your life through personal creative expression, no matter how insignificant it may seem. This opens the floodgate to full creative self-expression.

I open my creative self-expression to remove self-restrictions.

Day Three

Do you feel restricted in your leadership role? Do you have someone above you holding you down, or someone below you pulling you back? Perhaps even someone on each side of you is pulling you back and forth? Remove the restriction by stepping out, even if it is through volunteer or community work. Consciously move your leadership energy. Regardless of how insignificant the initial step may appear, this anchors your leadership abilities into physical reality.

I remove my leadership restrictions.

Day Four

Does someone or something restrict your mobility? Is there some-where you want to go or some way you want to get there, that simply is not falling into place? Mobility means movement. What in your life are you not allowing to move? Do you have clogged drains, pipes, stagnant water, restriction of air flow, air vents or filters that need cleaning, a muscle or tendon that is immobile? Release anything that is not moving as intended or anything that is "stuck" in your life.

I move through life without restriction.

Day Five

Do you have a need for emotional expression, but are restricted in your outlets? Do you restrict your feelings by internalizing them, leading to an unhealthy mind or body? Do you externalize your feel-ings in an incorrect manner? You can express yourself on the Over-soul level to release your restrictions of emotional expression.

I release my restrictions of emotional expression.

Day Six

Do you feel restricted in your ability to love and be loved? Do you have a lot of love to give but no one who appreciates this or per-haps no one at all? Why do you restrict the recipients of your love? Do you have an inability to love yourself? Are you worthy of being loved? Are you afraid of loving or being loved? How do you re-strict the flow of love, and why?

I release my restrictions on love.

Day Seven

Is your ability to communicate restricted? Do you often wish that you did/did not say something? Are you confused about what to communicate, with whom to communicate, and/or how to com-municate? Do you feel that your ideas are not fully appreciated? Do you use the tool of Oversoul communication? Do you visualize the color ice blue at the throat chakra surrounded by maroon for courage to improve your communication abilities?

I release my restrictions on communication.

I move through life without restriction.

Safety

Day One

Safety of Self is an ongoing issue, regardless of the world status. All experience is an outpicturing of your inner world. Nothing can happen to you unless there is a part of Self that attracts that type of experience. While it is important not to be paranoid, using common sense in everyday living is important. What are you doing to be safe in your environment?

I am always safe.

Day Two

Knowing that you are safe is paramount to the safety of your family and friends. Because all experience is an outpicturing of your inner world, nothing can happen to anyone else unless there is a part of you that attracts that type of experience. Do you worry excessively about the safety of others?

My family and friends are safe.

Day Three

Do you have concern for the safety of your assets, whatever they may be? God-Mind is limitless. With the correct mind-pattern know that you always draw to you everything that you need. This may not be what you want, but you will be taken care of in the way that is the best for the evolution of your soul-personality. Take a few moments to thank your Oversoul and God-Mind for all assets that you have and all assets that you receive.

All my assets are safe.

Day Four

Do you have concern about the safety of your pets? As with all things, what happens with your pets is an outpicturing of your mind-pattern. Nothing can happen to your pets unless on some level there is an agreement between all involved. Worrying about your pets attracts unsafe experiences to them.

My pets are safe.

Day Five

No matter where you go, from stepping out your front door, to traveling around the world, there is always the possibility that something could happen. There are even incidents of people sitting at home in the "safety" of their living rooms when cars or airplanes actually crash into these people! What do you allow into your life when you step out your front door, or for that matter, when you are comfortably settled at home?

I am safe wherever I am.

Day Six

Review your internal issues to proactively balance any part of Self that pulls you out of your center. Examine the deepest aspects of Self to find and release any part of the mind-pattern that does not operate from a place of safety.

All aspects of my Self operate from a place of safety.

Day Seven

Keep in mind that there are no safe places, only safe people. This means that no matter what is going on around you, with the correct mind-pattern you can walk through anything that comes your way with ease and safety. Use common sense as well as your Oversoul and Hyperspace protection techniques. Release any holes in your mind-pattern that might attract reactive situations. Recognize that you are always in the correct place at the correct time for you.

I am a safe person.

I am safe wherever I am.

Secret Knowledge

Day One

Have you been sidetracked by the proliferation of disinformation? If so, now is the time to narrow your focus so that you can move into the myriad of secret knowledge available. Take the time to go through your belongings, such as books, products, devices, and collectibles to see what kind of disinformation you may have in your possession. Now is the time to remove them from your environment so you can open yourself up to the next layer of knowledge.

I am ready to receive the next layer of secret knowledge.

Day Two

Recognize that you are full of secret knowledge not yet accessed. Breathe yourself into your center; align Self with Oversoul and God-Mind. Focus your consciousness at your pineal gland. Feel your storehouse of secret knowledge surfacing from the depths of your being.

My storehouse of secret knowledge surfaces from my depths.

Day Three

Focus on the outer world. The outer world is full of secret knowledge that is hidden in plain sight, right in front of your eyes. Recognize that everything that you see has at least three layers of meaning. Ask your Oversoul to bring these layers of meaning into your conscious mind.

I see the secret knowledge hidden in plain sight.

Day Four
Listen to the Earth to understand the geological secrets that she contains. Use color, tone, and archetype to guide your exploration of hills, mountains, lakes, streams, caves, and tunnels.
I understand the secret geological knowledge of the Earth.

Day Five
Align Self with Oversoul and God-Mind to understand the true history of humankind. Move through the outer layers of falsehood and into the secret knowledge buried within it. Flush out secret historical knowledge.
I flush out secret historical knowledge.

Day Six
What is going on behind the political scene? Who tells the truth? Who merely plays out a script from behind the scenes? Are there really multi-political viewpoints? Who perpetuates which illusions and for what purposes? Use color, tone, and archetype to go behind the scenes to understand secret political knowledge.
Secret political knowledge is now revealed to me.

Day Seven
What is the alien agenda? Move your consciousness around the globe to search out human consciousness and alien consciousness. Where is each located? Are they compatible? Project your consciousness out into the universe. What do you find and where? What kind of secret alien knowledge do you find?
Secret alien knowledge is now revealed to me.

I flush out secret historical knowledge.

Self-Correction

Day One

Every day, your soul-personality diligently works to correct you whenever you stray from your goals. Self-correct in conscious awareness so that you can reach your goals in the quickest, least uncomfortable way while acquiring the greatest amount of knowledge. For example, your physical body is your vehicle in this reality. Just like you want to drive the perfect car, create and operate the perfect body. Consciously self-correct your physical body into your perfect vehicle.

> *My physical body self-corrects into my perfect vehicle.*

Day Two

Whatever you study, for whatever reason, make the best use of your resources—time, energy, and funds. Allow your mind-pattern to self-correct so that it brings the best resources to you.

> *My mind-pattern self-corrects to bring me the best resources.*

Day Three

Allow your emotional issues to self-correct. Rather than fight the process, determine the easiest and least painful route through your experiences. When something does not go your way, this may be a sign to go another direction. Why continue to fight a losing battle simply because you know how?

> *My emotions self-correct.*

Day Four

As you sift through the proliferation of disinformation on your spiritual journey, recognize that your soul-personality knows what is truth versus what is not. Rather than listen to everybody else, ask your Oversoul to direct the self-correction of your spiritual journey so that you remain on the most focused path to reach your inner goals.

My Oversoul directs my self-correction.

Day Five

Self-correction may require some short-term upheavals to give you a better long-term outcome. Once you accept the process of self-correction, you understand that the short-term upheavals are worth the benefits.

I accept the process of self-correction.

Day Six

When your outer world is complicated and unsatisfying, ask your Oversoul to speed up the self-correction process. This may lengthen your short-term period of discomfort, but if you hang on through the bumpy ride, the results will outweigh the discomfort.

My Oversoul speeds up the self-correction process.

Day Seven

Use the process of self-correction in any area of your life where you feel stuck. On some level of awareness, you know exactly what you need. Sometimes it is difficult to "see the forest for the trees." Move yourself through the blind spots by allowing that part of you that already knows, to self-correct. Step aside, and be prepared for the changes.

My life now self-corrects.

I accept the process of self-correction.

Sexuality

Day One

Sexuality is usually publicly presented in a titillating manner that keeps people tied into their lower chakra bands. Mentally look at your root chakra band to determine if it is in bright red, rather than the balance of pale red. Release all the excess red up to your Oversoul until you see only pale red in that chakra band.

My root chakra band is pale red.

Day Two

Because the root chakra band is purposefully bombarded from outside sources on a daily basis, most people do not even realize that this chakra band is out of balance. Most people are so over-stimulated that the abnormal now seems normal. When this chakra band is over-stimulated, there is easy entry into the energetic system. Whenever you feel sexually stimulated, check to see if the color of this chakra band is bright red. If so, release the bright red up to your Oversoul until the color returns to pale red. This keeps your energetic system balanced and closed to outside influence.

I close my energetic system to outside influence.

Day Three

Some people have an excess of bright red energy in the root chakra band because of old hurts, beliefs, and disappointments. This can range from others not living up to relationship expectations to emotional and physical rapes. Mentally look to see if you have any old emotions tied into this area that need to be cleaned up and released.

My root chakra is now clear of old emotions.

Day Four

As you clean up the root chakra band and return it to balance, there is a higher likelihood of having a sexual relationship that is elevating instead of animalistic. Anyone can have sex, but without emotional attachment, it is devoid of deeper meaning.

I allow an elevating sexual relationship in my life.

Day Five

Sexual intimacy means emotional intimacy. People are accustomed to putting up fronts that do not allow emotional intimacy. Going from one relationship to another stops emotional intimacy. Stopping emotional intimacy stops your intimate relationship with yourself. Think about past sexual relationships in relationship to emotional commitment. Have you had, or do you have now, the level of emotional intimacy that you desire?

I now have an emotionally intimate sexual relationship.

Day Six

If you do not have any past sexual relationships, but would like one, then it is important to set everything in motion now. Make a list of what has stopped you in the past, such as fear, parents, low self-worth, weight, and/or inexperience. Focus on releasing these issues so that you can move through your own blockades. There is someone for everyone. Once you lift self-imposed blockades someone who matches exactly what you need will be able to come into your life.

I release all self-imposed sexual blockades.

Day Seven

No matter who you are, as long as you exist on this planet in human form, there will be sexual issues. These issues push you into places of yourself that literally touch you in very deep, private, and sensitive ways. Sexuality teaches you about yourself and the essence of creation in negative or positive ways—one way or another, in this lifeline, or another, you will learn. Choose to make this a positive experience.

I accept only positive sexuality experiences.

I release all self-imposed sexual blockades.

Simplicity Part I

Day One

Complex lives are distractions that keep the body, mind, and soul continually busy without allowing time for vertical movement and growth. Replace complexity with simplicity to redirect your life.

I replace complexity with simplicity to redirect in my life.

Day Two

Allow simplicity to permeate all facets of your life. This lightens the load that you carry on a daily basis.

I allow simplicity to permeate all facets of my life.

Day Three

Simplicity allows you to remove tension from your life. You breathe easier, you relax, and you have relief from your stress and tension.

Simplicity provides relaxation.

Day Four

As you relax with simplicity, the flow from Oversoul and God-Mind more easily enters your conscious mind. Now, solutions to your life challenges can more easily reach you.

Simplicity brings solutions to my life challenges.

Day Five

Simplicity allows your life to flow smoothly. You are relaxed, new solutions to life challenges present themselves, and now life flows smoothly.

Simplicity allows my life to flow smoothly.

Day Six

Simplicity means less distractions, allowing your thoughts to become more focused and directed. Simplicity strips away all that you do not need so that you can see what you do need.

My thoughts are focused and directed with simplicity.

Day Seven

Simplicity is the key to staying on your internal path to Self. Everything that you need to know becomes clearer and makes more sense.

Simplicity maintains my internal path to Self.

Simplicity maintains my internal path to Self.

Simplicity Part II

Day One

Finding out who you are may mean first finding out who you are not. Now is the time to remove all that is not you so that you can see what is left. Begin with your environment. Remove all objects that are not you —such as anything that annoys you, is difficult to use, or comes from others who you do not like.

I simplify my living environment.

Day Two

Are you following any complicated diets or eating regimens? Are you eating food without any nutritive value? Do you eat certain foods because you think that you "should"? What can you do to simplify your diet in a wholesome way that is healthy, nutritious, and relatively easy?

I simplify my diet.

Day Three

Do you feel that you meet yourself coming and going some days, if not most? What can you eliminate and/or streamline to make yourself feel like a person again?

I simplify my schedule.

Day Four

Do you find yourself overwhelmed with debt and/or expenses? What can you do to simplify your finances? Take another job? Downsize your needs? Expand your mind-pattern?

I simplify my finances.

Day Five

Are your relationships complicated? Do you need to take a permanent or temporary break from any of them? Do you need a physical and/or emotional time out?

I simplify my relationships.

Day Six

Do you have books, magazines, periodicals, or flyers, that you are going to read or might need some day? Area you reading from so many different sources that you feel confused by them all?

I simplify my reading materials.

Day Seven

Are you following too many different conflicting philosophies? If so, choose one or two that are compatible to explore.

I simplify my philosophical explorations.

I simplify my relationships.

Simultaneous Existences

Day One

In True Reality, there is no such thing as time and space. Everything happens at once. Your experiences depend upon your focus. To understand your current mind-patterns and their origins, as well as develop an appreciation for the richness of your soul-personality, it is sometimes necessary to look at alternate realities and timelines. Changing your focus changes your perception of who and what you are, allowing you to realize the depth and wealth of information to which you have access.

I explore the vastness of my soul-personality.

Day Two

Develop an awareness of the many simultaneous directions that your soul explores. Think about your current profession, whatever that may be. Close your eyes and follow it from its inception to its current phase to how you perceive its future. Realize that whatever you think with your thoughts, you create. You are creating right now, and some part of you is experiencing it. Why do you think you chose your profession? Or did it seem to choose you? What does your profession represent?

I simultaneously encompass past, present, and future.

Day Three

What other countries and places catch your attention, both positively and negatively? Have you made an effort to visit them? If not, have you read books, watched videos and movies about/from these places? Have you listened to music of other countries and places? What is your emotional response? Follow your emotions. Ask your Oversoul to shift your focus. Feel yourself there. Do you feel different when you energetically connect to these places? Who are you and why are you there?

I know my connections to other places.

Day Four

Are you drawn to other time periods? What captures your attention? Do you collect memorabilia, decorate from a specific era, or even like to dress according to other times? Close your eyes and feel what draws you there. Where are you and what are you doing? What kind of issues connect you to these timelines?

I know my past, present, and future connections.

Day Five

People in your life can be connected to you through alternate realities/timelines. Who catches your attention and how—both positively and negatively? Follow their energies to determine the relationships. Why are these people important to you now? When did the relationships really begin? Move your consciousness through the linear past and future to explore how they are all interconnected, keeping in mind the countries and timelines you previously explored. What repeated themes do you find?

I know my simultaneous relationship connections.

Day Six

Part-time hobbies are a residual of a full-time activity somewhere in your soul-personality. Follow your hobbies through linear time to find out who and what your soul is doing elsewhere. Allow your mind to expand in all directions to encompass the totality of your abilities and talents.

I know my simultaneous activities.

Day Seven

Realize that all your hopes, dreams, desires, and secret wishes are being played out by some part of your soul-personality right now. The moment you think, you create. Somewhere, some place, all the desires of your soul are now met. Focus on your desires to actualize them in this timeline.

All the desires of my soul are now met.

I explore the vastness of my soul-personality.

Speaking Up Part I

Day One

Are you able to speak up for yourself at the appropriate time in the appropriate way? Do you sometimes wonder why you said what you said, or wonder why you did not say something when you had the opportunity?

I speak up at the appropriate time in the appropriate way.

Day Two

Before you start to speak, do your breathing and centering work. Connect Self to Oversoul and God-Mind. Anchored in the strength of this triad, you can say what you need to say, when you need to say it.

I connect Self to Oversoul and God-Mind so that I can speak up.

Day Three

Wearing anything tight or restrictive at the throat is an outer reflection of restricting your words. This can be anything from neckties to jewelry to high collars. Remove these symbolic physical restrictions to help unleash your words.

I remove symbolic restrictions so that I can speak up.

Day Four

If you have the tendency to speak up at inappropriate times, mentally place a brown "X" on your throat. Use restrictive physical symbols to help hold your words in, such as neckties, jewelry, and high collars.

I speak up only when appropriate.

Day Five

All words have color. Use the correct color frequency when speaking to best convey your message. If you want to express calm, balanced emotions, use medium green. If you want to be understood, use pale yellow. Explore the colors for yourself.

I use color as an aid for speaking up.

Day Six

Before you speak with anyone for any reason, have a conversation with that person on the Oversoul level. This prepares the person for what you have to say, opening the pathway so that you can be heard.

I precede all conversations by speaking up on the Oversoul level first.

Day Seven

There are some people who do not want you to speak up. These people do not want to listen. Use the Oversoul level to reach these people. Yell and scream on the Oversoul level if you feel this is necessary. When you finally do have the opportunity to speak, your message will already have been received.

My Oversoul aids my ability to speak up and be heard.

I use color as an aid for speaking up.

Speaking Up Part II

Day One

Many people have issues about speaking up. Even though you may have an interesting opinion or something important to share, there is something internal that prevents you from sharing. Trace these feelings back to their origin to determine what prevents you from speaking up when it is appropriate. Go as far back as necessary to determine the origin of these feelings.

I understand why I do not speak up.

Day Two

When you suppress your words, there is a part of you that becomes frustrated and angry. As this part gets suppressed further inside, it has a need to express, and may do so inappropriately. For example, if you have a difficult day at work, you may come home and express your frustration by angrily speaking to your family. Have you had these kinds of experiences?

I speak up to the correct person at the correct time.

Day Three

Sometimes expressing what is on your mind is difficult, especially if it is a controversial or sensitive topic. To prepare yourself, balance your T-Bar archetype, spin your chakras in the correct sequence, place ice blue in your throat chakra band, and surround yourself in maroon for courage. Now, you are properly prepared to easily speak up!

I easily speak up when appropriate.

Day Four

If speaking up is difficult, practice speaking. Close the door to your room, look in the mirror, and speak. Say everything that is on your mind, releasing all to your Oversoul as you go. Become accustomed to the sound of your voice and know that it is okay to speak up and be heard.

I practice speaking up.

Day Five

You may have some sensitive issues that are weighing on your mind. Ask your Oversoul to direct your timing. Find a person with whom you can discuss these issues. Speak up and share. You may find that he/she has similar issues or experience. Simply speaking up helps to desensitize you from these issues, allowing you to view them with greater insight and objectivity.

I speak up about my most sensitive issues.

Day Six

If speaking up still seems difficult, write down your sensitive feelings. Keep a journal of what you would like to say. This helps move suppressed energy out of your system in some way.

I speak up through my written words.

Day Seven

Speak up for yourself using any method that works. The most important thing is that you speak the appropriate words to the appropriate people at the appropriate time. This is important to keep you mentally and physically healthy.

I speak up.

I understand why I do not speak up.

Stagnation

Day One
Just because life is busy and hectic does not necessarily mean that your life is moving forward. This simply means that life is busy and hectic. In fact, there may be parts of you that are stagnating, but you are so busy that you do not even see this. What areas of yourself and/or life do you consider to be stagnant?
I identify areas of stagnation within myself and life.

Day Two
Look around your environment to identify and observe specific people, places, and things that you consider stagnant. These are all reflections of you. Usually, the reflections are exaggerated outer expressions so that you can finally see what is going on inside of your, and correct it.
I identify outer reflections of my inner stagnation.

Day Three
Determine what part of yourself that these people, places, and things reflect. Rather than impatiently dismiss the reflection, use the reflection to teach you about you. Consider these reflections pieces of your personal puzzle. You are the detective who solves the hidden mystery.
I interpret the outer reflections of my inner stagnation.

Day Four
Recognize that inner pockets of stagnation keep the entire soul-personality from progressing. The soul-personality cannot move into its next level until it gets all of itself moving in the same direction. Look in the hidden corners of your environment for

clues. Do you have stagnant food in the refrigerator or freezer? Stagnant puddles of water in your yard? Stagnant bank accounts?

I remove hidden pockets of stagnation from my mind-pattern.

Day Five

Who do you know that you think most blocks your way in the outer world? That person represents your inner stagnation. Facing this person symbolically represents confronting your inner areas of stagnation. In person or on the Oversoul level, communicate with this person to determine how you can move through this block.

I confront my inner stagnation.

Day Six

Anything that consistently repeat, can lead to stagnation. Continually frequenting the same shops or businesses, eating the same foods, keeping the same routine, or visiting with the same people may be symbolic of inner stagnation. Stir up your usual routines to stir up your inner being.

I stir up my routines to stir up inner stagnation.

Day Seven

Break old habits and patterns that have become dull, routine, and boring. With a little creativity, you will be amazed at the dramatic growth that results. There are many craeative ways that you can break old, stagnant mind-patterns so that you can move forward into your potential.

I creatively break old, stagnant mind-patterns.

I confront my inner stagnation.

Step At A Time

Day One
When life seems overwhelming and you do not know what to do, take one step at a time. First, retreat from the big picture. Review one small piece of your life that is manageable. Then, slowly expand your vision until you find a very small area that needs attention. Focus on getting that one small piece of the puzzle in order before going on to the next small piece. Take one step at a time.

I take one step at a time to bring my life into order.

Day Two
If one step is too much, then take one-half step. If one-half step is too much, then take one-quarter step. Movement is important, because without movement you become stagnant. If you become stagnant, then your Oversoul will do something to force movement. For this reason, it is better to move slowly than not to move at all.

I take one-half step at a time to create movement.

Day Three
If you are not sure what even one-quarter of a step might be, then go back to your Oversoul and Hyperspace basics. Use your affirmations to determine your next step.

I now know the next step I need to take.

Day Four
If you still do not understand your next step, then take a step, even if you know it is not the most correct one. Moving incorrectly signals your Oversoul that you are going somewhere. Your Oversoul

will correct you one way or the other. You will receive direction on a more correct move. Now, you can begin inching forward.

I take one step at a time to determine my correct direction.

Day Five

Focus on the goal instead of the process. With your goal in mind, know that as long as you move forward step by step, you reach your goal.

I take one step at a time to reach my goal.

Day Six

Your Oversoul knows the steps you need to take. Even if you cannot logically understand the sequence, follow the guidance of your Oversoul.

My Oversoul guides me one step at a time.

Day Seven

As each step is accomplished, the next step is automatically revealed. By taking one step at a time, you learn to understand the process as you practice patience and inner trust.

As I accomplish one step, the next step is automatically revealed.

I take one step at a time to reach my goal.

Stop Self-Sabotage

Day One
Do you self-sabotage your goals? Do you set yourself up only to be knocked down again? Do you get close to your goal, but never reach it? Think about how many times, you were "almost there" but did not make it.
I release the need to self-sabotage.

Day Two
Do you do well for a few days, and then something happens to feed your doubts and worries? Do you pay too much attention to the negative comments of others? Do you suppress your doubts and worries instead of address them?
I release the need to self-sabotage via doubt and worry.

Day Three
Do you build a new mind-pattern only to have the strength fizzle out? Do you focus on your goal? Do you hold your goal at your pineal gland, continually feeding it with affirmations and correct action?
My affirmations pull me through self-sabotage.

Day Four
Review past mind-patterns and actions that kept you from attaining your goals. Do you have current mind-patterns that continue this trend? Are you ready to release the need for self-sabotaging mind-patterns?
I release the need for self-sabotaging mind-patterns.

Day Five

Do you draw people into your life who support your goals or who drain you of your life force? Do people say one thing but their actions show something else? Is it time to consider who you really want in your life and who you do not?

I attract people who help pull me through self-sabotage.

Day Six

Do you invite self-sabotaging experiences into your life? Do you go on a diet and then invite friends out to lunch? What are your goals and what seems to always stop you from reaching them? What kind of self-sabotaging trends have you developed?

I identify and release self-sabotaging trends.

Day Seven

With awareness and focus, clear the way to smoothly reach your goals instead of self-sabotaging along the way. Review your mind-patterns that create self-sabotage, releasing them as you go. With a new mind-pattern in place, you can release your self-sabotage mind-patterns now.

I now release all self-sabotage mind-patterns.

I identify and release self-sabotaging trends.

Strength

Day One

When the outer world exudes fear, despair, and hopelessness, it is easy to buy into this message, making this your own statement toward life. You are greater and grander than this message. Dig down deep inside; into your own internal strength. Move beyond this ludicrous and false message that emanates from the outer world.

I reach deep down inside into my own internal strength.

Day Two

You are strong. Feel your own inner strength coursing through your body, mind, and soul in every level of your being.

My inner strength courses through every aspect of my being.

Day Three

Allow the strength of your own resourcefulness to come to the surface. You are an unstoppable force. You already contain within you the solution to every situation that confronts you.

The strength of my resourcefulness guides me.

Day Four

Recognize the strength of your mind-pattern; what it creates and pulls to you. Know that properly directed, the strength of your mind-pattern can consciously pull you through any situation easily and comfortably.

The strength of my mind-pattern pulls me through all situations.

Day Five

You are one with the frequency of strength. Know this frequency inside and out, on all levels. Define it verbally, feel it physically, experience it energetically. Know the power that comes with strength. Release the fear of using strength incorrectly. Know the strength that permeates every cell of your being.

Strength permeates every cell of my being.

Day Six

Build your physical body to represent your mental body. A strong physical body symbolizes a strong mind. A strong physical body is imperative to hold and wield the strength of your mind.

My strong physical body symbolizes the strength of my mind.

Day Seven

Take time every day to anchor Self into the strength of your Oversoul and God-Mind. Anchored in this strength, you can face absolutely anything that comes your way.

I am anchored in the strength of my Oversoul and God-Mind.

Strength permeates every cell of my being.

Struggle

Day One

In what areas of your life are you struggling? Make a list, and think about how many weeks, months, or even years that you have been struggling. Do you enjoy learning this way?

I release the need for struggle.

Day Two

Prioritize your struggle list, from most difficult to least difficult. What is the least difficult struggle? What could you do differently to stop the struggle in that area of your life? Instead of talking, thinking, or trying, make a decision to just do it.

I stop the struggle.

Day Three

Where in your life do you unconsciously perpetuate the mind-pattern of struggle? Do you struggle with a stuck drawer, struggle to open a tight jar, struggle to get under a pile of papers, struggle with a jammed lock, or even struggle into a pair of pants? Struggle, struggle, struggle…change the smallest struggle that you can think of to imprint a mind-pattern free of struggle.

My mind-pattern is free of struggle.

Day Four

Do you struggle with a relationship? Is it time to end it, or do you enjoy the struggle? Stop the need for struggling and the relationship dissolves, or changes, of its own accord.

My relationships are free of struggle.

Day Five

Do you struggle with finances? Why do you need to participate in a financial struggle? Does this struggle enhance your low self-worth and self-esteem issues?

My finances are free of struggle.

Day Six

Do you struggle with relocation issues? Why do you need the struggle? Is it making you strong enough so that you can do what you need to do? Are you strong enough? Do you want to be? Why do you want to struggle?

I relocate without struggle.

Day Seven

You can keep the mind-pattern of struggling forever, as God-Mind allows all choices. Where will you be in your struggles tomorrow, next week, next month, next year, or even several years from now? Will you still be struggling with the same issues?

My life is free of struggle.

My life is free of struggle.

Sub-personalities

Day One

Everyone has a myriad of sub-personalities. These sub-personalities may be self-compartmentalizations, or they may have been externally created. Identify your sub-personalities. Begin with easy ones, such as wife, mother, daughter, husband, father, son, employee, and patron. Note how each sub-personality within Self interacts in a different way.

I understand the concept of sub-personalities.

Day Two

Do you have one overall outer sub-personality that communicates with the world, and one that runs your inner world? Why do you feel the need to do split yourself in two? Why not show the outer world who you are? If you lose some established friends and acquaintances, do you think new ones will enter into your life?

I blend my inner and outer sub-personalities.

Day Three

Do you have positive sub-personalities that sometimes control you? If so, what are they? Love? Peace? Wisdom? Kindness? For example, you can express love of food, ideals, and people in a negative way. You can have such a peaceful existence that you stagnate. What are the negative aspects of your positive sub-personalities? Are your positive sub-personalities in balance?

I identify my positive sub-personalities.

Day Four

Do you have negative sub-personalities that sometimes control you? If so, what are they? Anger? Impatience? Frustration? Guilt? Fear? What are the positive aspects of your negative sub-personalities? Are your negative sub-personalities in balance?

I identify my negative sub-personalities.

Day Five

What sub-personalities control you? How do they gain control? Where do you go when this happens? How do you regain control of Self?

I am in control of all sub-personalities.

Day Six

How did your sub-personalities develop through the years? What color are they? What substance comprises them? Can you identify the ones that are too weak? Too strong? Can you bring all of your sub-personalities into balance so that they work for the same goals instead of against one another?

My sub-personalities are in perfect balance.

Day Seven

Do you allow the outside world to feed your sub-personalities? For example, does your ego sub-personality receive gratification from others or from you? Does your anger sub-personality feed off the anger of others? Does your peace sub-personality feed off of the complacency of others?

My sub-personalities are internally maintained.

My sub-personalities are in perfect balance.

Suicide

Day One

Some people experience deep depression on a regular basis. This sometimes leads to contemplation of suicide. Suicide only succeeds in removing you from the physical body—you are still the same. You still have the same mind-pattern which continues to re-create the same experiences, except without a physical body.

I release all suicidal thoughts.

Day Two

Sometimes the depression you feel is not really yours—it is fed by the outer world. Create a mind-pattern that is impenetrable by the outer world. This way you are not susceptible to outside influence.

My mind-pattern is impenetrable by the outer world.

Day Three

Some people have suicide programming. If you have constant thoughts of suicide, this might be your issue. Constantly use the brown merger archetype to hold yourself together. This integrates any compartmentalized part of Self that wants to take over your mind. Use of this archetype helps you control all parts of Self at all times.

I merge and control all parts of Self.

Day Four

Pay attention to your environment and its effects upon you. Clean if necessary. Rearrange furniture. Choose uplifting colors for your clothing and décor. Walk for balance. Make a conscious effort to create an environment that is pleasant. Be around people who pull you up. Read enriching materials. Changing your environment changes your mind-pattern.

I create an uplifting environment.

Day Five

Reach out to others. If you feel alone, be assured that there are others who feel the same. If you internalize your deepest feelings, know that there are others who do the same. Use the strength of your mind-pattern to create a supportive network of people with whom you can be interdependent.

I now have a supportive network of people.

Day Six

Appreciate the physical body that you have created. Take care of it with correct food and exercise. Develop a relationship with your body so that you can understand its needs.

I take great care of my physical body.

Day Seven

You may feel yourself start to disassociate from this reality. Usually, something triggers this to make this happen. This closes the part of you that feels as you retreat into survival mode. Something is so painful that you do anything not to feel it. Or, your internal pain is so intense that you try to externalize the pain by physically harming your body. To counteract these actions, flood your entire being with medium green for emotional healing as well as pale pink for unconditional love of Self.

I love myself unconditionally.

I now have a supportive network of people.

Superhuman Abilities

Day One

Make a list of everything that you think holds you back from actualizing your potential, whether it is person, place, thing, or Self. How is everything on your list a reflection of you? To develop superhuman abilities, you first must surpass anything that holds you back.

I surpass my actuality to attain superhuman status.

Day Two

When you fight the human experience, you cannot attain the potential of being human, much less anything beyond. Be grateful for this lifeline and the human experiences that it brings.

I appreciate my human experience.

Day Three

In a simultaneous existence, you have already attained superhuman status. If you can visualize something, it already exists. Use the strength of your mind-pattern to focus on this simultaneous existence to bring it into this reality.

I focus on my superhuman simultaneous existence.

Day Four

Allow your physical body to operate at 100% capacity. This gives it superhuman status since most people only use approximately 3% of their DNA capacity.

My physical body operates at 100% capacity.

Day Five

Allow your mind to operate at 100% capacity. This gives it super-human status since most people only use approximately 10% of their mental capabilities.

My mind operates at 100% capacity.

Day Six

Can you handle superhuman status? What would you do with this type of power? Would you control it or would it control you? Would you be able to objectively and effectively use your superhuman abilities for the benefit of all humankind?

I use my superhuman abilities for the benefit of humankind.

Day Seven

The strength of your mind-pattern brings whatever you create. Decide with caution what you ask for, because you might get it. Appreciate the human experience first so that you can handle superhuman status. Choose superhuman status with wisdom so that your decision moves your only forward on your journey. Always remember that the higher you are, the harder you fall. Everyone is subject to this Universal Law.

I choose superhuman status with wisdom.

My mind operates at 100% capacity.

Support System

Day One
Everyone has a support system for body, mind, and spirit. What is yours? Does it support you in the way that you would like, or does it support old mind-patterns that are no longer necessary? Think about what kind of support system you have in place right now.
I label my current support system.

Day Two
Have discussed with your Oversoul exactly what kind of support system that you would like, its equivalent, or something better? Take the opportunity to build the support system that elevates you into your next level of development.
I now have an elevating support system.

Day Three
What does your physical body reflect of your support system? Is your spine supporting you in alignment? Do you need to visit a chiropractor for an "adjustment"? How about your feet—do they support you in your journey forward? How is your bone density and muscular system? What does your physical support system state about your life support system?
My physical support system is in balance.

Day Four
Have you tried cultivating a support system beyond your current one? Have you ventured from your own place of safety to pave the way for others to come to you? Do you allow a new support system to form?
I allow a new support system into my life.

Day Five

Do your spiritual beliefs provide you with the support that you need? Do you have adequate spiritual support? Do you have a great spiritual support system?

I have a great spiritual support system.

Day Six

If you can envision a support system, it exists somewhere. With the strength of your mind-pattern, bring it to you.

The strength of my mind-pattern pulls my support system to me.

Day Seven

Interpret the communication from your Oversoul in new and different ways. What you seek may not come to you exactly as you envision. Your support system might be a breath away. Look beyond the obvious or you may totally miss it. The least obvious person might be the one with the most to offer. Review your surroundings—you might be surprised by what you find.

I recognize my support system.

I now have an elevating support system.

Survival

Day One
Many people question their reasons for existence in this reality. Some react to the influence of ELF, mass mind-control, and internal self-sabotage programs, all designed to create a robotic society. Everyone chose to be here for a reason. This includes you.

I survive in this reality for a reason.

Day Two
When people get into their emotional levels, they sometimes forget the logical aspects of their existence. Because you are here for a reason, should you choose to leave prematurely, all levels of your soul-personality would be in jeopardy.

I survive all circumstances.

Day Three
Everyone who is here has diligently worked to create their unique set of personal circumstances, regardless of perceived level of difficulty. Because you set up this set of circumstances, it is in your best interest to explore your own creations in this reality. Surviving means you exploring you.

I survive my self-created life circumstances.

Day Four
Keep yourself in balance so that you can survive your self-created life circumstances in the least uncomfortable way possible.

I survive my life in balance.

Day Five

Whether you want to admit it or not, you have at least one personal mission here. You need to survive so you can complete the many layers of your personal mission.

I survive to complete my personal mission.

Day Six

Your soul-personality needs this set of circumstances for specific reasons. These circumstances bring balance to the overall soul-personality. What you set up here is important to Self, Oversoul, and God-Mind. Your survival is important to the fulfillment of the needs of your soul-personality.

I survive to fulfill the needs of Self, Oversoul, and God-Mind.

Day Seven

You play a part in this reality that no one else can fulfill. If you are not here, then your part leaves a void, disrupting all other roles in progress.

I survive to fulfill my part in this reality.

I survive in this reality for a reason.

Thanksgiving

Day One

It is easy to think of the things that you are supposed to be thankful for, like food and shelter. What about being thankful for some things you may not appreciate? For instance, look at your home and think about its upkeep. How do you feel about cleaning your home? Do you ever complain about it? Without a home, you would have less work to do!

I am thankful that I have a home to maintain.

Day Two

Mondays are not always easy days. For many people, Mondays signify the end personal time and the start of work time. Mondays also provide a focal point which gives your life order and organization.

I am thankful for the organization my daily routine provides.

Day Three

Just think, without income, you would not have any bills to pay. Be grateful for your bills!

I am thankful for my bills.

Day Four

Do you feel rushed and overwhelmed as you prepare for holidays, however you celebrate them? Perhaps finishing up at work, food and household preparations, extra traffic, long lines? If you did not have any holidays, you would not feel rushed and overwhelmed! Enjoy the process!

I am thankful when I am rushed and overwhelmed.

Day Five

Family holidays can be stressful. Families are made up of all kinds of people, most likely none of them perfect. Who do you seeing at family gatherings that you prefer to avoid? What part of you do these people reflect?

I am thankful for the people who reflect me.

Day Six

Do you eat too much at holiday gatherings? Do you eat too much or put on weight?

I am thankful that I have all the food I need.

Day Seven

How many people in the world would gladly trade their life for yours? Maybe it is because you have shelter, food, transportation, relationships, employment, medical care, education, personal growth, and all the issues that come with these opportunities.

I am thankful for all that I have.

I am thankful for the people who reflect me.

Toning

Day One

Toning is one of the easiest tools of change, but often the least used and understood. Toning is sound replication—"playing" the sounds in and around you. Most people feel self-conscious when singing, so go into your shower, turn the water on, open your mouth, and listen to what comes out.

I explore through tone.

Day Two

Each soul-personality is a frequency which is comprised of its one unique tone. These tones are created through experience. For example, sad experiences create one set of tones, happy experiences create another set of tones. Whatever comes out of your mouth is the current layer of tone that currently expresses through you. This is the beginning of the Song of Your Soul.

I tone the first layer of the Song of My Soul.

Day Three

Play your body like a musical instrument. Start at your feet and work your way up through the top of your head. What sound does each part of your body express? What story is contained within each sound? How does the toning make your body feel?

I play the tones of my physical body.

Day Four

Toning can shatter old mind-patterns. Focus your concentration at your pineal gland. Use tones to shatter all old, stagnant, non-serving mind-patterns. Ask your Oversoul for explanation as you go.

My tones shatter old-mind patterns.

Day Five

Toning can install new mind-patterns. Use tones to rearrange, create, and install new mind-patterns that uplift you to vertical movement.

I tone to install new mind-patterns.

Day Six

Now that you have had a chance to express your soul's journey through sound, shattered old non-serving mind-patterns, and installed new ones, tone your current layer of the Song of Your Soul. Observe how this layer is different from the first layer.

I tone my current layer of the Song of My Soul.

Day Seven

You can tone to bring your current goals to fruition. Focus your goals at your pineal gland. Ask your Oversoul to give you specific tones to bring these goals to fruition.

My tones bring my goals to fruition.

I explore through tone.

True History

Day One

What is true history? What is the mind-pattern that keeps it hidden from you? What is the mind-pattern that reveals it to you? Create a mind-pattern that reveals true history.

My mind-pattern reveals true history.

Day Two

Do you recognize the falsehoods in history as it is currently taught? Do you recognize the bits and pieces of true history that you can follow?

I discern true history from false history.

Day Three

Do you observe true history for yourself? When you travel to historical sites, do you take the time to discern what is false and what is true? Do you explore the frequency of the area to determine true history?

My frequency research determines true history.

Day Four

Do you visit with others who have access to true history? Do you listen to what others say happened? Do you separate fact from fiction?

I find the facts of true history.

Day Five

Do you study legends and myths to add to your knowledge of true history? Do you think about why legends and myths survive and perpetuate? Who were the storytellers of bygone days? Why do the legends and myths survive?

I find true history in legends and myths.

Day Six

Do you look for trends and patterns to help dig out true history? Do you observe how current history-in-the-making is distorted or skewed for one reason or another? Do you think about how this time period will be recorded in history? Will you be able to help keep true history alive?

I help keep true history alive.

Day Seven

Do you observe on all levels to determine true history? Are you able to put the complete picture together so that you have a better understanding of true history versus recorded history? Do you understand why histories have been distorted?

I gain my own knowledge of true history.

I help keep true history alive.

Trust

Day One

Trusting others can be a challenge. Sometimes, people whom you have trusted for long periods of time do things that make you doubt who and what they are. On the Oversoul level, mentally put these people in pale orange to see if they are speaking/doing the truth. Put yourself in pale orange so that you can only hear the truth.

I sort out whom to trust.

Day Two

Trusting information can be a challenge. There are so many sides to every story, that it may seem impossible to sort fact from fiction. On the Oversoul level, place the information in pale orange. Place yourself in pale orange so that you can easily discern the truth.

I know which information to trust.

Day Three

The most important person to trust is you. Everything else out-pictures your personal level of self-trust. What situations have you been in where you did not trust your own abilities? Or, are there situations where you trusted yourself and later realized you could have done something differently? Have you trusted others only to find out that you could have listened to yourself with better results? Are you willing to walk through the "mistakes" in order to reach into a level of self-trust?

I trust myself.

Day Four

How do you build self-trust? Begin by aligning Self, Oversoul, and God-Mind, and moving into your center. Place the entire alignment in pale orange and move forward as best as you can. If something undesired happens, realize that you stepped outside the pale orange. Breathe yourself back into your center and recreate the alignment.

I trust the alignment of Self, Oversoul, and God-Mind.

Day Five

Trusting the process may seem difficult when you think that you cannot see the light at the end of the tunnel. However, just because you do not immediately see the end does not mean that it does not exist. To imprint trust of the process, get a map and plot a route that you have never taken before. Either mentally, or with a vehicle, explore the route. Enjoy the side trips, but make a decision to go the most direct route to reach your destination. Understand that the trip to reach your goal is as important as the goal itself.

I trust the process.

Day Six

Trusting your decisions can be challenging. There are certain situations where you wish that someone would make the decision for you. If you have made some decisions with negative consequences, this makes the decision-making even more challenging. When your decision-making involves major life changes, this presents another set of challenges. Trust that whatever decision you make leads you on the path that is the best for the evolution of your soul-personality.

I trust my decisions.

Day Seven

Specifically target any areas of your life lacking trust. These are all reflections of your inner Self. This is your unique and interesting puzzle—to find out what part of Self that this reflects back to you. Continue to search for clues until the big picture makes sense.

My environment reflects my trust of Self.

I trust myself.

Truth

Day One

With the proliferation of information is a mountain of disinformation. Disinformation is false information mixed with enough of the truth to catch your attention. Wound around the truth are other colors that take you wherever your mind cares to wander. Recognize truth by its pale orange color.

I discern truth by its color.

Day Two

Truth has a tone to it. When you are ready to hear it, truth sounds wholesome and complete. Disinformation sounds harsh and incomplete. The tone of truth is a constant.

I discern truth by its tone.

Day Three

Truth has an archetype associated with it. Ask your Oversoul to show you the base archetype for truth. Place this archetype over any information that you question. See if the information contains this archetype. If so, does all of the information contain it, or only portions? If only portions, which portions?

I recognize truth by its archetype.

Day Four

Discern the frequency of truth for yourself. Begin by asking questions that allow you to feel the truth in the answer. For example, what is your name? Where do you live? What are your favorite activities? When you answer these questions, you know that you are telling the truth. Identify the underlying feeling of truth.

I recognize the feeling of truth.

Day Five

Disinformation is full of holes, puffs of smoke, darkness, and deceit. Identify what this deceit feels like. Identify its color, tone, and archetype. Feel how it winds its way around the truth. As you identify disinformation, you strip it away to find the truth hidden within.

I clearly identify truth.

Day Six

Practice your disinformation detecting techniques. Start with newspapers and books. Hold them, feel them, and allow your mind to swirl in and around them. Know that you know truth from fiction. Know what is important to assimilate and what you need to discard.

I know truth from fiction.

Day Seven

Practice your disinformation detecting techniques. Listen when others speak. Listen to when the words do and do not match the feelings of the people. Pay attention to how you actually feel, not how you think that you should feel based upon the reactions of others or previously gathered information. Do not judge or criticize, merely observe and gather the truth.

I observe and understand the truth in all life situations.

I clearly identify truth.

Undercurrents

Day One
Every life is filled with undercurrents. These are the little irritations and annoyances that prevent you from fully enjoying your present moment. Rather than avoid these undercurrents, pay attention so that you can complete them once and for all.
I complete the undercurrents of my life.

Day Two
Search out any little thing that troubles you so that it can be corrected. These little things are uncomfortable undercurrents that pervade all that you do. Take care of the little things so that they do not grow into big things.
All my undercurrents rise to the surface.

Day Three
If you only smooth out undercurrents, they repeatedly return. This means that you continue to spend your energy fixing the same thing. Rather than quick-fix these undercurrents, pull them out, deal with them, complete them, and let them go. Decide to stop dealing with the same situations over and over again.
I effectively remove all undercurrents from my life.

Day Four
Do you have any relationships that flow smoothly on the surface, but have undercurrents of discord? This can be anything from family and friends to co-workers. Discuss the situation with these people on the Oversoul level. Then, if necessary, discuss the situation in person. Release these undercurrents from all relationships.
I release the undercurrents in my relationships.

Day Five

Do you have areas of your home that need to be cleaned out or organized that you have been putting off? Or perhaps you get started, but only go "so far?" Make a decision to complete this task, so that it is no longer an undercurrent of unpleasantness and discomfort in your life.

I release the undercurrents in my environment.

Day Six

Do you have any uncompleted projects tucked away or even staring at you openly? Completing these projects removes the undercurrent of discomfort; that nagging feeling of something left undone. Whatever you start, you must in some way complete, or you will always have a nagging undercurrent hanging onto you.

I release the undercurrents of uncompleted projects.

Day Seven

Look in every nook and cranny of your being to find any undercurrents that leave you unfulfilled, unsatisfied, or unsettled in any way. Finalize and complete these undercurrents so that they do not continue to follow you wherever you go, whatever you do. Now is the time to just do it!

All undercurrents in my life are now gone.

I complete the undercurrents of my life.

Unification

Day One

Any fragments that you see in the outside world are symbolic of fragments of yourself that are not united. Do you have anything broken in your environment that needs to be fixed? If so, now is the time to fix it, while contemplating its inner symbolism.

I unify my inner fragments.

Day Two

Do you have any relationships that you see as broken? These represent inner relationships that are broken. How can you unify these relationships? Do you have to give up something to unify them? Is it within reason? If you give up something, will it change you? If so, how?

I unify my relationships to unify my Self.

Day Three

Developing compassion for others changes your life. When you feel compassion for others' fear, ignorance, and stagnation, you feel compassion for your own journey. Compassion aids in the unification of old, broken pieces into a new and stronger whole.

Compassion unifies old pieces into a stronger whole.

Day Four

Are your finances fragmented and in need of unification? What do your finances represent? Can you consolidate debt and credit cards? Do you need to change your financial institution? Do you need to take care of old debts that you have let go? Unify your finances so that you can unify your own inner resources.

I unify my finances to unify my inner resources.

Day Five

Do you take the time to clarify and unify your emotions when in conflict? Do you have one emotion that leads the rest, such as anger or fear? Do you address each emotion to fully understand the concerns of the soul-personality in its totality? Allow all parts of you to express so that you can unify your emotions. Now, you can move forward easily and effectively to resolve all conflict that comes your way.

I unify my emotions.

Day Six

Do you take the time to unify your left and right-brain hemispheres? Breathe yourself into your center. Breathe out through the top of your head up into your Oversoul. Go for a walk. Balance logic with emotion. All of these techniques create unification of left and right-brain hemispheres.

I unify my left and right-brain hemispheres.

Day Seven

Do you take the time to unify Self, Oversoul, and God-Mind? Do you take the time to recognize this trinity of your existence? The deeper your alignment and unification of Self, Oversoul, and God-Mind, the more consistent unification reflects back to you from the outer world.

I unify Self, Oversoul, and God-Mind.

I unify my inner fragments.

Uniqueness

Day One

Rather than focus on how to fit in with others on their terms, acknowledge your own uniqueness. Understand your own terms and be true to them.

I am true to my own uniqueness.

Day Two

You have a unique path, different from the path of anyone else. You unique path has developed a strength that is unique to you. Your uniqueness contains your strength.

In my uniqueness I find my strength.

Day Three

The deeper you go into your own uniqueness, the more answers you find. These answers may not make sense to others because these are your answers. These answers are exactly what you need for success on your own unique path.

I find all my answers within my uniqueness.

Day Four

Allow your mind-pattern to bring you an income stream that allows your uniqueness to shine. The more you tap into your uniqueness, the more self-satisfaction and contentment you feel within and without.

My income stream allows my uniqueness to shine.

Day Five

Allow your mind-pattern to bring relationships to you that accept your uniqueness. If you change yourself to match the expectations of others, you will never be self-satisfied or content in your life.

All my relationships accept my uniqueness.

Day Six

View your uniqueness as an advantage in your creative thought process. You see solutions where others only see blocks. Value your contributions wherever you go, regardless of input from others. Receive your validation from within.

I view my uniqueness as an advantage.

Day Seven

Acceptance and understanding the uniqueness of Self allows you to accept and understand the uniqueness of others. The circle is complete–what you give out returns to you.

I accept and understand the uniqueness within others.

I am true to my own uniqueness.

Vertical Growth

Day One

The outer world is designed to create horizontal movement. This means that you continually repeat the same experiences without resolution. How do you move horizontally? How many times do you repeat the same experience in different ways?

I release the need for horizontal movement.

Day Two

Vertical growth means moving inward and upward into new growth. Do you continually ask the same questions to different people? Instead of asking the same questions, develop new questions. New questions mean new answers that pull you up into vertical growth.

My new questions pull me up into vertical growth.

Day Three

Do you read the same types of books but written by different people? Do they provide anything different, or is the same information presented in the same way? Choose two or three complementary authors. Reread their books to glean new levels of understanding. Vertical growth means new experiences and new information. In this way, explore Self, Oversoul, and God-Mind in new and exciting ways that continues to pull you up into vertical growth.

I read for vertical growth.

Day Four

Do you go to the same places - the same parking spot, grocery store, restaurant, or recreational area? Going to the same places in the outer world means you go to the same places in your inner world. To create vertical growth, go to different places. Decide if these places are only horizontal movement of if they bring you vertical growth.

I choose vertical growth in all my activities.

Day Five

Weight issues often result from horizontal movement. Continual horizontal movement means that your physical structure out-pictures what the mind is doing.   Many overweight people carry weight that is not theirs as they reach out horizontally. They encompass the energy of others, bringing it back into their own auric fields. Moving your energy vertically allows you to pull your energy up. This releases any weight belonging to others that you may be energetically holding onto.

I choose vertical growth to release horizontal weight gain.

Day Six

The way you spend your leisure time can pull you out into horizontal growth. Incorporate new and different leisure activities to grow vertically. You may want to have separate activities for the body, mind, emotions, and spirit. Realize when you have fully explored each activity. Then, move upward into a new level of this activity or another one.

My leisure activities move me up into vertical growth.

Day Seven

Vertical growth takes you into new levels of Self, Oversoul, and God-Mind. In turn, each new level leads you into the next, each more exciting and fulfilling than the last. Appreciate the exploration process – it is endless and exists for your enjoyment.

I enjoy my upward journey into vertical growth.

I choose vertical growth in all my activities.

Victim-Mentality

Day One
Do you sometimes feel like you wear a sign on the front that says, "Hit me," and one on your back that says, "Kick me in the rear"? Make a list of people who take take advantage of you now, or who have done so in the past. The Earth plane has a tendency to attract soul-personalities with victim-mentalities – this is one reason why you are here.
I release the need for a victim- mentality.

Day Two
Do you wind up in situations that drain and exhaust you because you say "yes" when you want to say "no"? Speak up for yourself. Put your throat chakra in ice blue. Surround this with maroon for courage. Practice saying, "I'll think about it." Then, think about it.
I speak up to end victim-mentality.

Day Three
Have you had any major victimizations in your life? Why did they happen? What could you have done differently? What will you never do again? What weaknesses in your mind-pattern need correction to prevent this, or a similar situation, from occurring? What was in your mind-pattern that allowed this to happen?
Victim-mentality teaches me about my mind-pattern.

Day Four

What minor victimizations happened to you? Have you waited in line only to have someone else helped first, received a late credit card charge because your payment arrived one day past the due date, heard someone say something nasty as you turned to leave, bought something at one price only to have the clerk ring it up at a higher price? How many times have you thought, "Here we go again," but let it go because you did not have the time, energy, or courage to correct the situation?

I immediately correct victim-mentality experiences.

Day Five

Visualize the victim-mentality mind-pattern as a plant with long roots growing inside of you. Pull that plant out by its roots, giving it all up to your Oversoul.

I pull out the roots of my victim-mentality mind-pattern.

Day Six

Who consistently contributes to your victim-mentality mind-pattern? Do release work with that person via the Oversoul level. Then, call or visit this person. How do you react? Is your victim-mentality dissipating?

My victim-mentality is gone.

Day Seven

Review the many ways that you have been a victim. What did victim-mentality teach you? What are you changing so that you permanently release this mind-pattern? Because the Earth plane attracts people with victim-mentality, this is your opportunity to finally overcome this mind-pattern. In doing so, you help others who follow in your footsteps.

I help others surpass victim-mentality.

My victim-mentality is gone.

Vision

Day One
Do you want to know what is in store for you? Do you want to know where to go, what to do, who to visit, when to make your next move? Then pay attention to what is going on right now. Look at everything that is around you right now. Improving your outer vision improves your inner vision. Put your eyes in the color royal blue for 45 seconds. Clean a window to see more clearly on all levels.

I see with clarity.

Day Two
Sit in a comfortable chair. Observe your surroundings. Are your surroundings pleasant? Organized? Disorganized? Cluttered? Dusty? Dead plants? What do you see? Put your eyes in the color royal blue for 45 seconds. Clean your contacts, glasses, or sunglasses with baking soda, a gentle cleanser that removes the most stubborn dirt. See your surroundings with clarity.

I see my surroundings with clarity.

Day Three
Take a walk, or look out a window. What do you see? Objectively observe the weather, people, foliage, animals, and colors. Be aware of all that exists. Look for details that you may have overlooked. Put your eyes in the color royal blue for 45 seconds. Clean a mirror to see life's reflections with clarity.

I see life's reflections with clarity.

Day Four

Sit in a comfortable chair. Sit up straight, hold your head still, and allow only your eyes to move. Without moving your head, look up toward the ceiling as far as you can. Look to your right, then to your left. Now, look down toward the floor. Roll your eyes around one direction, then the opposite way. Squeeze your eyes close, then quickly open them wide. Put your eyes in the color royal blue for 45 seconds. Clean the windshield on your car so you can see your journey in life with clarity.

I exercise my outer eyes to improve my inner vision.

Day Five

Sit in a comfortable chair. Drop your shoulder muscles. Loosen your neck muscles by moving your head slowly side to side, then down toward your chest. Lean your head back. Repeat as often as you wish. Put your eyes in the color royal blue for 45 seconds. Clean your computer screen to communicate with clarity.

I have accurate outer and inner vision.

Day Six

Look at the sun at sunrise or sunset. Slowly turn your head from left to right, right to left while keeping your eyes focused on the rising or setting sun. Feel the eye muscles relax. Put your eyes in the color royal blue for 45 seconds. Clean your television screen to view the world that you invite into your life with clarity.

I see what I invite into my life with clarity.

Day Seven

Close your eyes. Focus your attention at your pineal gland between the eyebrows. Put your eyes in the color of deep royal blue. Feel the depth of your inner vision pierce through all barriers. Align your inner vision with your Oversoul and God-Mind. See with clarity all that presents itself.

My inner vision is strong, deep, and clear.

I see with clarity.

Vortices

Day One

There are vortices all over the Earth. A vortex can be a person, place, thing, or even mental state. These vortices exist for many different reasons. Some are positive, some are negative, but each one can transport you to other areas within yourself.

I identify all vortices.

Day Two

Physical vortices are sometimes referred to as power points. These power points amplify energies, either positively or negatively. What feels positive for you may affect another person negatively, depending upon your mind-pattern. If you feel that you are in a vortex, determine its affect.

I pull positive vortices to myself.

Day Three

You can get locked into a mental vortex. This is what happens to people who get into a depressed state. A negative mind-pattern is pulled into a mental vortex. No matter what you do, this swirling vortex sucks you further and further down into it. When you feel this way, do your best to release all the negativity up to your Oversoul. This creates a reverse pull that releases you from your mental vortex.

I reverse the pull of negative vortices.

Day Four

As you release negative vortices, fill the void with violet. This protects and filters out the negative influence.

I fill all negative vortices with violet for protection.

Day Five

Vortices can trigger internal programming. Keep the brown merger symbol at your pineal gland to stay centered and focused. Make notes of feelings, thoughts, and dreams based upon vortex symbolism, including such things as tornadoes, black holes, vacuums, and drains.

I am aware of vortex symbolism.

Day Six

Observe your reactions to vortex symbolism. Determine solutions to counteract any negative reactions. For example, if you see a spinning tornado, then with your mind, spin the tornado in the opposite direction. If you feel a black hole or vacuum sucking you into it, then reverse its pull to springboard you into the opposite direction. Use your own creative talents to reverse whatever is needed.

I utilize all vortices to my advantage.

Day Seven

Proactively create your own upward spinning vortex into your Oversoul and up into God-Mind. Understand the vortices within and without so that you take control of yourself before something else takes control of you.

I create my own vortex into my Oversoul and God-Mind.

I am aware of vortex symbolism.

Walking

Day One
Take time every day to walk for pleasure, if possible. Walking is an important aspect of your life. If you cannot take a physical walk, then take a few minutes to take a mental walk somewhere pleasant and uplifting.

I enjoy walking.

Day Two
Walking balances your body.   Feel the process as the physical body balances, aligns, oxygenates, and stretches.

Walking balances my body.

Day Three
Oxygenation sustains the human organism, aerating the entire system so that all energetic processes flow smoothly and evenly through the physical structure. Visualize medium green flowing through your body to aerate every cell in your system.

Walking aerates my entire system.

Day Four
Walking strengthens your muscles—muscles allow movement. Create movement in the physical structure and the mind-pattern changes accordingly. As the body progresses, so does the mind.

Walking strengthens my muscles and mind.

Day Five
Walking increases your bone density. Your bones are your support structure. Tthis reflects in your mind-pattern that says you are now supported in all areas of life.

Walking increases my support system.

Day Six

Walking is great to balance your brain. Left, right; left, right; this constant movement balances emotion and logic, physical and non-physical, internal and external; positive and negative.

Walking balances my brain.

Day Seven

Walking gives you private time for deep thinking. Your brain is the most oxygen intensive organ in your body. Deep breathing means deep thinking. A balanced brain means balanced conclusions. Experience for yourself on all levels the benefit of walking.

Walking gives me private time for deep thinking.

Walking increases my support system.

War

Day One
How do you feel about war? If there is war in the world, then there must be some kind of internal warring faction within your own mind-pattern. Where within yourself are you waging an internal war?

I identify my own internal war.

Day Two
Are you geographically close to a war? This indicates the strength of your own internal war. The closer to the war you are geographically, the stronger the internal war. Release your own internal wars up to your Oversoul and God-Mind.

I release my internal wars up to my Oversoul and God-Mind.

Day Three
Are you directly participating in war? How you participate says something about your level of internal war. Are you at the front lines fighting, providing administrative support, medical support, supply provider, or have family or friends in these positions? Understand the symbolism of your participation. Your personal involvement with war tells you something about you.

I understand my involvement with war.

Day Four
Bravely face your own internal wars. Enumerate what they are and how they started. Facing your issues helps the outer world face its issues. Resolving your internal wars must be reflected in the outer world.

I face my internal wars.

Day Five

Are you marching for peace, or would you like to? Then, some-where inside you are marching for peace. Let your own thoughts, feelings, emotions, and experiences come together in peace so that you can end your internal war.

I bring peace to my internal wars.

Day Six

Do you pray for peace? Prayer means that you are looking for answers from your Oversoul and God-Mind to end your internal wars. Be ready to receive the answers that you need to conclude your internal wars.

Prayerful answers conclude my internal wars.

Day Seven

Do you think that people in the world have the resolution to war? Do you think that they know what to do, but do not put this into practice? This means that you have the answers but do not know how to utilize them. In other words, you know how to make internal peace, but for some reason, you refuse. Utilize what you know. What you see in others is a reflection of yourself.

My own internal wars now end.

I bring peace to my internal wars.

Weight

Day One
People who have inner voids often try to fill these voids with food. This means that you need to be emotionally nourished. Until your emotional void is filled, you will keep overeating. This is an attempt to compensate for lack of emotional nourishment. Whenever you feel emotional voids, mentally fill them with medium green for emotional nourishment.

I now have emotional nourishment.

Day Two
Sometimes you eat because you feel lonely and isolated, regardless of how many people are around you. Observe when you eat only because you feel the need for companionship and sharing. Stop eating. Mentally fill your void with pale pink for unconditional love of Self.

I now have unconditional love of Self.

Day Three
Sometimes people cannot gain or maintain weight no matter how hard they try. This represents a mind-pattern of not slowing down to fully appreciate the experiences of physical reality. This can also represent a mind-pattern of not utilizing and learning from the experiences that you have. Both mind-patterns mean that you are trying to escape from this reality.

I fully participate in physical reality.

Day Four

Sometimes you do not eat because you refuse to be a part of physical reality. This represents refusing to ingest the experiences that physical reality offers. Sometimes you do not eat because on some level you simply do not want to be here. In effect, you are committing a slow and painful suicide by allowing yourself to waste away. Even if the body no longer exists, you do. In or out of body, your lessons are the same.

I honor my commitment to exist in physical reality.

Day Five

Sometimes overweight people eat very little, but still gain weight. Sometimes underweight people eat voracious amounts yet cannot gain anything. Even at your correct weight, your digestive system may not be functioning properly. Mentally flood the digestive system in pale yellow to maintain efficiency.

I use pale yellow to maintain my digestive system.

Day Six

One reason why people overeat is because their bodies are hungry even though their stomachs are full. You can be overweight, underweight, and even at your correct weight, and be undernourished. Eating the correct combinations of foods for your body represents the correct combination of thinking in your mind. Do you put food into your mouth that nourishes your body? Do you think thoughts that nourish your mind?

I properly nourish my mind and body.

Day Seven

Observe your eating habits. Recognize the nourishment you require for body, mind, and soul. When these are in balance, you will be at your perfect weight. All journeys begin with one small step. Create the perfect weight for your body.

I create the perfect weight for my body.

I now have unconditional love of Self.

Appendix:

You Have The Answers

The challenges in your life did not just happen. They evolved through a series of actions that you set up over a course of time. On some level of awareness, you created them, so that you could learn and grow from them. Because you created them, you have the knowledge to dismantle them. All you have to do is work backwards. When you are in the middle of a challenge, it can be difficult to assess where you are, how you got there, and what you can do to get out of it. You may relate to the old saying, "You can't see the forest for the trees."

Recognize Specific Actions
You need a tool to help you recognize the specific actions that have created your challenges. Once you know what those actions are, then you can determine where you are, how you got there, and what you can do to get out of it. Affirmations are powerful and useful tools that bring specific answers to specific questions forward into your conscious mind. An affirmation is a statement that defines a course of action, or a state of inner being. Repeating affirmations many times by thinking, speaking, or writing can bring new avenues of action into your conscious mind.

Using Affirmations
Both your positive and negative actions almost always combine together into patterns that create your challenges. Recognizing this, the affirmations that you choose provide answers that you can accept and utilize. As an example, you may be experiencing a difficult relationship with your son. Your first thought might be that you try your hardest, and you do not understand why he acts the way that he does toward you. Slow down and remember that your outer world is a reflection of you. Then ask the question, "What am I doing that is being reflected back to me by my son?" No matter how hard you think, you may not be able to come up with an answer.

You Already Know

An affirmation can bring that answer into your conscious mind, because on some level of awareness you already know. Start with a basic affirmation that states the basic problem and your willingness to resolve it:

> *I am willing to release the conditions that create a negative relationship with my son.*

To put the affirmation into motion, think of it throughout your day, speak it out loud if you wish, and most effectively, write it a minimum of ten times daily. Because you are willing to release the conditions, they will surface up from your aura, up from your subconscious mind, and out of your physical body, where they have been buried. On their way out, they pass through your conscious mind. This identifies those conditions for you.

Positive And Negative Actions

Because both your positive and negative actions have combined into a pattern of behavior to create your present challenge, expect both positive and negative actions to surface into your conscious mind. For example, you may learn that you tried to gain your son's love and approval by controlling and manipulating him. Wanting his love is a positive action. Your attempt to gain it through control and manipulation is a negative action. He resents your interference, and now he is rebelling.

You may learn that you always criticize and correct him to "make him a better person." Wanting him to be a better person is a positive action. Criticizing and correcting to make him one is a negative action. He may not appreciate that, and expresses his disapproval through actions against you. Or, perhaps you are still angry with him over specific childhood incidents. You try not to feel angry at him. That is a positive action. But, on some level, your anger still exists. That is a negative action. On some level, he feels and reacts to your anger.

Remember, there is no need to judge or criticize yourself when you identify these patterns of behavior. Realistically, you are where you are supposed to be with the tools, knowledge, and experience that you have. Be thankful that you are facing these parts of yourself so that you can learn from them, release them, and make specific changes.

Release The Conditions
Now that you are aware of the conditions that create the negative relationship, release them with the following affirmation:

I release the conditions that create a negative relationship with my son.

You may want to release specific conditions, because they also create other negative relationships. Use one or more affirmations from the following subset:

I am willing to release my need to be controlling and manipulative.

I am willing to release my need to criticize and correct.

I am willing to release my need for anger.

Prepare For The New
As those aspects are released, prepare for a new relationship with your son. Change your affirmation to the following:

I am willing to accept a positive relationship with my son.

To enhance that positive relationship, use this subset of affirmations:

I allow my son to be who he wants to be.

I allow myself to have relationships centered around positive experiences.

As your relationship improves, continue to change your affirmation to fit your present:

I accept a positive relationship with my son.

And, finally, change it one last time to pull you into a positive relationship with your son:

> *I now have a positive relationship with my son.*

A Part Of The Process

Initially, this may look like a lot of work, and, in a way, it is. But, your relationship did not get to be the way it is overnight. It developed over many years. So, take the time to effect a long-lasting change instead of looking for a quick fix. Eventually, you will enjoy searching out the conditions and making the changes. It is all a part of the process:

> You create a negative relationship.
> You dismantle the negative relationship.
> You create a positive relationship.

Affirmations Bridge Gaps

You may also need to design a series of affirmations to bridge the gap between what is, and what you want to be. For example, if your body is experiencing illness, you may choose the following affirmation:

> *I have a healthy body.*

You may want to believe that your body is healthy, and you may try to believe that it is healthy, but this is not your reality. If your body is not experiencing health, it may be difficult to convince your conscious mind that it is. You may feel an internal struggle as you try to convince yourself that it is healthy. At the end of this chapter you will find an example of a series of affirmations for a healthy body that you can use to help bridge the gap between your current and future reality.

A Five Step Process

When you are working hard to find an answer to a challenge that has you baffled, there is a process of designing affirmations that will maximize their effectiveness. It consists of the following five steps:

1. Find out what conditions are causing your present situation.
2. Release the old conditions.
3. Prepare yourself to accept the new conditions.
4. Accept the new conditions.
5. Affirm your new condition.

Utilizing these steps prepare the soil to accept the seed. If the soil is not properly cultivated, fertilized, and watered, the seed will have difficulty taking root. This is an extremely effective process, and the results are long-lasting.

Writing Affirmations

The most effective way to utilize affirmations is to write them. Get a notebook with lots of paper, and allow yourself a few minutes every day to write the affirmation that you have chosen. If possible, set a specific time, such as first thing in the morning, or before you go to bed at night. Establish a routine that helps you follow through with your goals. Writing affirmations may be a challenge in the beginning, but your results will encourage you. Experiment with different affirmations to find the ones that feel right at the time. Finding affirmations that work for you becomes easier with practice. There are some short and simple affirmations in the appendices that you might enjoy using.

Design Your Own

There is also a guideline for designing your own affirmations at the end of this chapter, followed by some examples. Start with the first one in the series, and write it a minimum of ten times daily. If you think about it during the day, repeat it silently or out loud. When you feel comfortable that you have fully utilized the first affirmation, and have received answers that make sense to you, move on to the next affirmation in the series. In addition, work with the subset that you have developed. You will know when it is time to move on to the next one. The more times that you write each affirmation, the faster you bring answers into your conscious mind. You may find that you do not have to use all five steps. You may be able to use two or three steps, depending on your challenge.

Affirmations Evolve

Eventually, your affirmations evolve on their own as you use the process. You do not have to think about the next step—it automatically occurs. One day, while writing your current affirmation, you may feel like changing it. You automatically flow with what is right for you—as a unique individual with a unique path into yourself. Affirmations bring very immediate results. They teach you that you already have the answers. You, along with your Oversoul and God-Mind, can find any answer that you need. All that is necessary to get started is a few minutes a day, a piece of paper, a pen, and an open mind that allows you to try.

Guideline For Designing Affirmations
Using the following five step process, develop a series of affirmations that work for you. Start with the first affirmation, and when you are satisfied with the information that you have brought forward, then design your second one. When the second one has brought the answers forward that you need, then design your third, etc.

1. Find out what conditions are causing your present situation:
      I am willing to release the conditions that create…
Make a list of those conditions as they come into your conscious mind.

2. Release the old conditions:
      I release the conditions that create…
           Develop a subset of affirmations.

3. Prepare yourself to accept the new conditions:
      I am willing to accept…
           Develop another subset of affirmations.

4. Accept the new conditions:
      I accept…

5. Affirm your new condition:
      I now am/have…

Affirmations For A Healthy Body
1. I am willing to release the conditions that create illness.

This affirmation brings the conditions that create illness into your conscious mind.

Those conditions might be:

> It gives me extra attention from family and friends.
>
> It gives me a chance to talk about myself.

It teaches me how to take care of my body through negative learning.

2. I release the conditions that create illness.

You may need a subset of affirmations:

> I release the need for negative attention.
>
> I release the need to learn about my body in a negative way.
>
> I release the need for (specific thought and behavior patterns that create my specific illness).

3. I am willing to accept a healthy body.

You may need another subset of affirmations:

> I am willing to accept positive attention.
>
> I am willing to learn about my body in a positive way.
>
> I am willing to change (specific thought and behavior patterns that create my specific illness).

4. I accept a healthy body.

5. I now have a healthy body.

Affirmations For Abundance

1. I am willing to release the conditions that create lack.

This affirmation brings the conditions that create lack into your conscious mind. Those conditions might be:

> My mother told me I would never amount to much.
>
> Other people experience abundance, but it won't happen to me.
>
> I am not worthy of abundance.
>
> I do not deserve abundance.

2. I release the conditions that create lack.

> Your subset of affirmations becomes:
>
> > I forgive my mother for her words.
> >
> > I forgive myself for believing them.

I am a worthwhile and deserving person.

3. I am willing to accept abundance.

> Your next subset of affirmations becomes:
>> I am worthy of abundance.
>> I deserve abundance.

4. I accept abundance.

5. I now experience abundance.

Affirmations For Positive Relationships

1. I am willing to release the conditions that create negative relationships.

This affirmation brings the conditions that create negative relationships into your conscious mind. Those conditions might be:

> I am controlling and manipulative.
> I am complaining and criticizing.
> I hold inner hostility toward people in my life.

2. I release the conditions that create negative relationships.
Your subset of affirmations becomes:

> I am willing to release my need to be controlling and manipulative.
> I am willing to release my need to complain and criticize.
> I am willing to release my need to be hostile.

3. I am willing to accept positive relationships.
Your next subset of affirmations becomes:

> I allow everyone to be who each wants to be.
> I allow myself to have relationships centered around positive experiences.

4. I accept positive relationships.

5. I now have positive relationships.

Chapter excerpt from *Decoding Your Life: An Experiential Course in Self-Reintegration* by Janet D. Swerdlow, Expansions Publishing Company, Inc., © 2005, pages 23-29

Glossary

ACTIVATION: When a program is brought to full function.

AFFIRMATION: A statement that defines a course of action, or a state of inner being; repeating words many times by thinking, speaking, or writing it to bring new avenues of action into your conscious mind.

ALTER: Section or compartmentalized personality within a programming matrix.

ARCHETYPE: Symbol or glyph from hyperspace or mind-patterns.

AURA: Your personal energy field.

CENTER: Your center is aligned along your spine, providing a safe space from which to work; you pull yourself into it by willing yourself into it.

CHAKRA BAND: Energy center of the body and encompassing area.

CHAKRAS: Along the human spinal column there are main nerve bundles called ganglions, which are esoterically called "chakras," a word which means "wheels" in Sanskrit. They form along the "S" curve of the spine which looks like a snake. For this reason the chakra system is referred to as "Kundalini," the Sanskrit word for snake.

COLLECTIVE CONSCIOUS MIND: The body of space that contains the accumulated known knowledge of humankind.

COLLECTIVE UNCONSCIOUS: The body of space that contains the accumulated thoughts of humankind; these established thought patterns directly affect what you move through today.

CONSCIOUS MIND: Contains your present.

DEPROGRAMMING: Techniques to block and/or remove mind-control/programming.

DIRECT AWARENESS: To know by experiencing the knowledge.

DNA SEQUENCES: This refers to the DNA sequences opening up in the body which is a form of Kundalini activation. DNA codes are the instructions that tell your body what to do and be. Some instructions you are running at birth. These dictate that you will have blue eyes, two legs, two arms, etc. Others activate later in life, such as health conditions, ability to play music, sing, etc.

ENERGY: A physical substance consisting of shape, weight, consistency, and color.

ELF: Extra low frequency generally related to microwaves for mind-control purposes; energy waves that influence body and mind.

FREQUENCY: A rate of vibration that distinguishes one flow of energy from all other flows.

GOD-MIND: Neutral energy; All That Is.

GROUP-MIND: Formed when vibrations band together.

HABIT RESPONSE: An established pattern of behavior that allows you to react to any given situation without thinking, whether physical or mental, it can be positive, negative, or neutral.

HORIZONTAL EXPERIENCE: Pulls you out into similar growth.

HYPERSPACE: A region of consciousness that exists outside of linear space and time.

ILLUSION: The way you perceive things to be.

KNOW BY KNOWING: To understand through direct awareness; to understand the feeling of an experience.

KNOWLEDGE: Information.

LANGUAGE OF HYPERSPACE: The Original Language that emanates from the Mind of God consisting of color, tone, and archetype (symbol).

LOVE: Neutral energy that emanates from God-Mind that does not discriminate.

MACROCOSM: God-Mind; All That Is; the larger picture of everything.

MEDITATION: A process that moves you beyond words and con¬nects you with silence, the level of feeling; the listening from which information is gathered; centered in the right-brain.

MICROCOSM: You; a world in miniature.

MIND-PATTERN: Blueprint of a person's thoughts.

NEGATIVE: Negative is not "bad," but merely a condition that exists; the opposite of positive, which explains another part of the same experience.

OBJECTIVE LISTENING: Listening and evaluating without judgment or criticism.

OBJECTIVE OBSERVING: Watching and evaluating without judgment or criticism.

OVERSOUL: Neutral energy that comes out of God-Mind; your Oversoul is to you what your Earth parents are to your body. Your Oversoul is your point of origin out of God-Mind.

PINEAL GLAND: Organ at the center of the head.

POSITIVE: Positive is not better than negative, but is merely a condition that exists; the opposite of negative, which explains another part of the same experience.

PRAYER: Request that affects the results of meditation; centered in the left-brain.

PROACTIVE LEARNING: Active learning; gathering knowledge before an experience occurs.

PSYCHIC ENERGY: Your personal energy; it flows back and forth, and is horizontal.

REACTIVE LEARNING: Passive learning; gathering knowledge after an experience occurs.

REALITY: The way things really are; it may vary considerably from your perception of the way you think things are.

SILENCE: The deepest level of inner awareness; the level of feeling; you connect with your Oversoul and God-Mind within silence.

SIMULTANEOUS EXISTENCE: All lifelines occurring at the same moment in the Eternal Now.

SPIRITUALITY: A state of inner being.

SOUL-PERSONALITY: Individual strand of an Oversoul.

SUBCONSCIOUS MIND: Contains your memories, moment by moment, lifeline by lifeline.

SUB-PERSONALITY: A group of similar emotions that bcomes strong enough to develop its own consciousness; a subpersonality is not you, but it is a part of you.

SUPERCONSCIOUS MIND: Provides the direct link to your Oversoul and God-Mind.

T-BAR: Archetype emanating from the pineal gland relating to balance.

TRIGGER: Sensory input that opens a program.

UNIVERSAL ENERGY: Energy that is available to everyone; using it allows you to keep your psychic energy; it flows up and down, and is vertical.

UNIVERSAL LAW: Rules and regulations that pervade all creation; emanates from God-Mind.

VERTICAL EXPERIENCE: Pulls you up into new growth.

VIBRATION: Frequency rate of an energy.

VIBRATORY IMPRINT: Accumulated feelings of like experi ences; they cause you to react to your experiences of today through your accumulated feelings of yesterday.

VISUALIZATION: Creating a mental scenario that can be mani fested either mentally or physically; centered at the pineal gland.

WISDOM: Knowledge applied.

YOU: Individualized neutral energy.

Index

D

Y

Expansions Publishing Company, Inc.
Products and Services
www.expansions.com

Addressing The Issues

Montauk: Alien Connection

Blue Blood True Blood: Conflict & Creation

True Reality of Sexuality

Stewart Says…

<u>Additional Books</u>

White Owl Legends: An Archetypal Story of Creation

Belief Systems Shattered

Belief Systems Shattered…Again

DVDs

**Advanced Hyperspace, Oversoul &
Deprogramming Techniques**

DNA, Galactic History & You

Simultaneous Existences

History of Mind-Control

Mind-Control & Programming Parts I & II

Deprogramming for Counselors

Sexuality, Ritual & Relationships

Illuminati & Montauk

Montauk: One Man's Story

**Conspiracy Con: From Mind-Control to Mind-Patrol &
The Reptilian Agenda**

True world History Series

Finding The Solutions

Healer's Handbook: A Journey Into Hyperspace

Hyperspace Helper: A User-Friendly Guide

Decoding Your Life:
An Experiential Course in Self-Reintegration

13 -Cubed
Case Studies in Mind-Control & Programming

Life Support Group ™ Manual
Self, Members, or Leaders

DVDs

Oversoul & Hyperspace Basics

Dream Analysis & Intermediate Color Codes

Basic & Intermediate Color Codes

Triad Healing

Nonhuman Communication

Nonhuman Chakra & Energy Systems

Scanning

Survivor/Surpassor

Mind/Body Correlations

Intuition Intensive

Level II Includes:
- Nonhuman Communication
- Nonhuman Chakra & Energy Systems
- Scanning
- Survvor/Surpasser

Level III Includes:
- History of Mind-Control
- Mind-Control & Programming Part I
- Mind-Control & Programming Part II
- Deprogramming Techniques for Counselors
- Sexuality, Ritual, & Relationships
- Mind/Body Correlations

Personal Consultations with Stewart & Janet

Monthly Newsletters

Janet's Planet

Stew's News

Visit
www.expansions.com

Read the Newest Cutting-Edge Information

Daily Practical Tips

Current Events & News

Q & A Column

Articles by Janet and Stewart

Newsletter Subscriptions
Stew's News
Janet's Planet

Latest Books, DVD's, & Products

Seminars, Lectures, & Events
...and Much More!